Carom Billiards: Cushion First Patterns

3-Cushion Billiards Championship Shots

From International Competitions
(Test Yourself against Professional Players)

Allan P. Sand
PBIA Certified Instructor

ISBN 978-1-62505-226-1
PRINT 7x10

ISBN 978-1-62505-418-0
PRINT 8.5x11

First edition

Published by Billiard Gods Productions.

Santa Clara, CA 95051

U.S.A.

For the latest information about books and videos, go to: http://www.billiardgods.com

Acknowledgements

Wei Chao created the software that was used to create these graphics.

Table of Contents

Other books by the author …

    3 Cushion Billiards Championship Shots (a series)

    Carom Billiards: Some Riddles & Puzzles

    Carom Billiards: MORE Riddles & Puzzles

    Why Pool Hustlers Win

    Table Map Library

    Safety Toolbox

    Cue Ball Control Cheat Sheets

    Advanced Cue Ball Control Self-Testing Program

    Drills & Exercises for Pool & Pocket Billiards

    The Art of War versus The Art of Pool

    The Psychology of Losing – Tricks, Traps & Sharks

    The Art of Team Coaching

    The Art of Personal Competition

    The Art of Politics & Campaigning

    The Art of Marketing & Promotion

    Kitchen God's Guide for Single Guys

Introduction

This is one of a series of Carom Billiards books that show how professional players select shots, based on the table layout. All of these shots have been mapped out based on shots played at international competitions.

This book contains a wide variety of examples where the player shot the Cue Ball (CB) into the cushion(s) before the CB hit the first Object Ball (OB).

These shots put you inside the head of the player beginning with the ball positions (shown in the first table layout). The second table layout shows the shooting decision and the results of the player's choice.

About the Graphic Layouts

There are two graphics for each shot. The first graphic shows the ball positions on the table. The ball labeled "A" is always the player's CB. The first graphic the ball positions on the table. The second graphic shows how the shot was played.

Each table graphic in this book is a black & white representation of a standard 5 x 10 carom billiards table. Balls are represented with these three symbols.

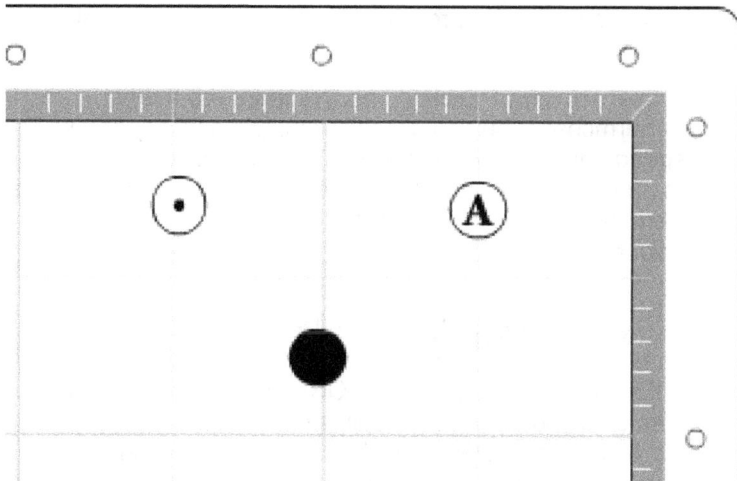

(A) The white "A" ball "A" is ALWAYS the shooter's cue ball.

(·) The white "center dot" ball is always the opponent's cue ball.

● This is the red Object Ball, represented in the layouts as the black ball.

Each shot is represented with two layouts on each page. The first layout shows the ball position setup BEFORE the shot. The second layout shows the ball pathways that the balls travel during the shot.

Table Setup

1. Use donuts (paper reinforcement rings) to mark positions for the carom balls. These are available at any office supply store.

2. Place chalk cubes at the locations where the CB contacts each rail.

When you play the shot, observe where the CB pattern and each rail contact. You may need several attempts as you make adjustments to the CB spin to properly follow the pattern.

Purpose of the Layouts

These are examples of shots that champion 3-cushion players from all over the world had to play. The first graphic provides the layout. The second graphic provides the results of their shooting solution. These layouts are provided for two purposes.

*   Use the first layout as a mental exercise. The player picked one, but there are many possibilities. From the comfort of your armchair, you can consider multiple options, and work out the pattern using the spin and speed you would have applied. These help stretch and extend your skills in tactical analysis. Then consider how the player decided how to shoot the shot. From the patterns you can determine how the CB was played and the type of applied spin. It's helpful to use a pointer (or your finger) to trace the pattern as you work out how the shot was played.

*   The second purpose is to take these layouts to the practice table. Position the paper reinforcement rings in place for each ball. You are going to shoot the layout many times, so these donuts help mark the ball positions for each attempt. BEFORE you experiment with your own "solutions", shoot the pattern until you can easily duplicate the paths. This means you will do a lot of experimentation to find the spin/speed used by the original player. Only AFTER you understand and can execute the pattern should you experiment with your own ideas.

This combination of mental analysis and practical table practice will boost your growth as an intelligent and thinking carom billiards player.

A: 1 Cushion

On these shots, the CB goes into one rail first and then into the first OB. The CB then contacts two (or more) rails and then into the second OB for the point.

A: Group 1

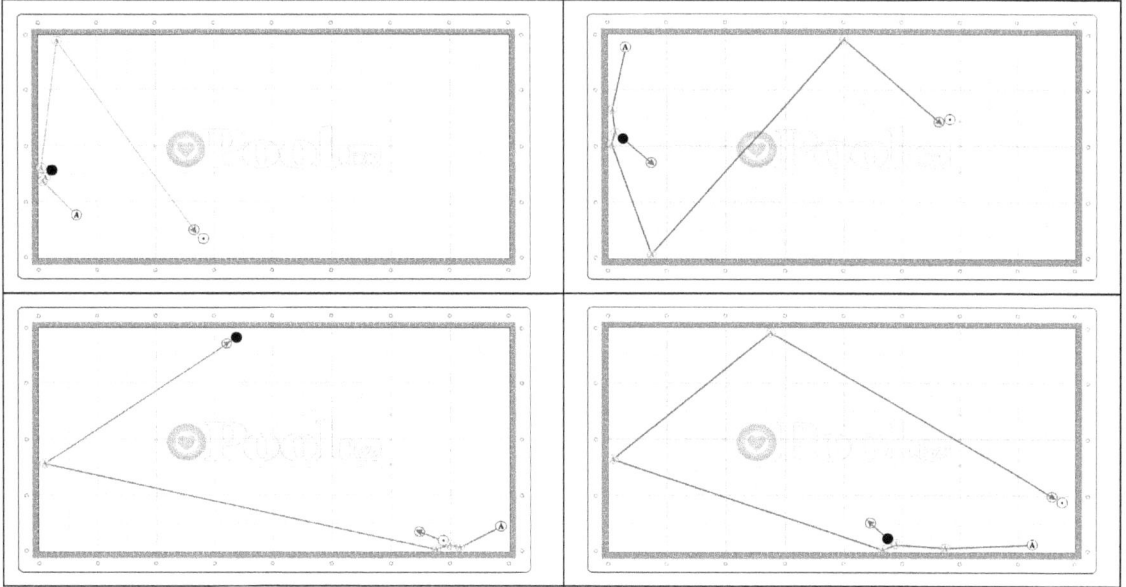

Analysis:

A:1a. _____

A:1b. _____

A:1c. _____

A:1d. _____

A:1a – Setup

Shot Pattern

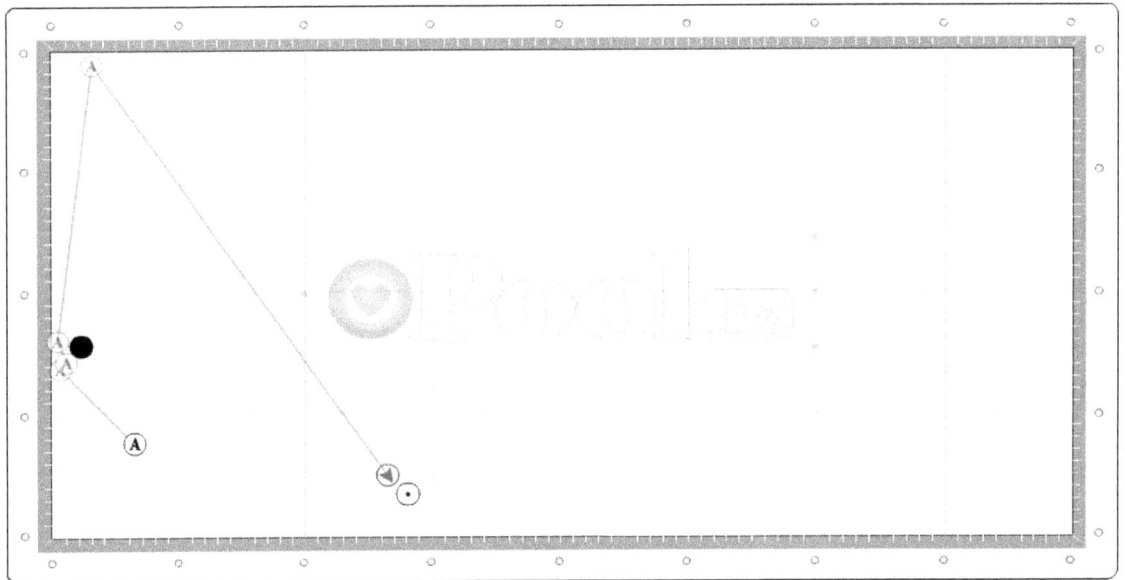

A:1b – Setup

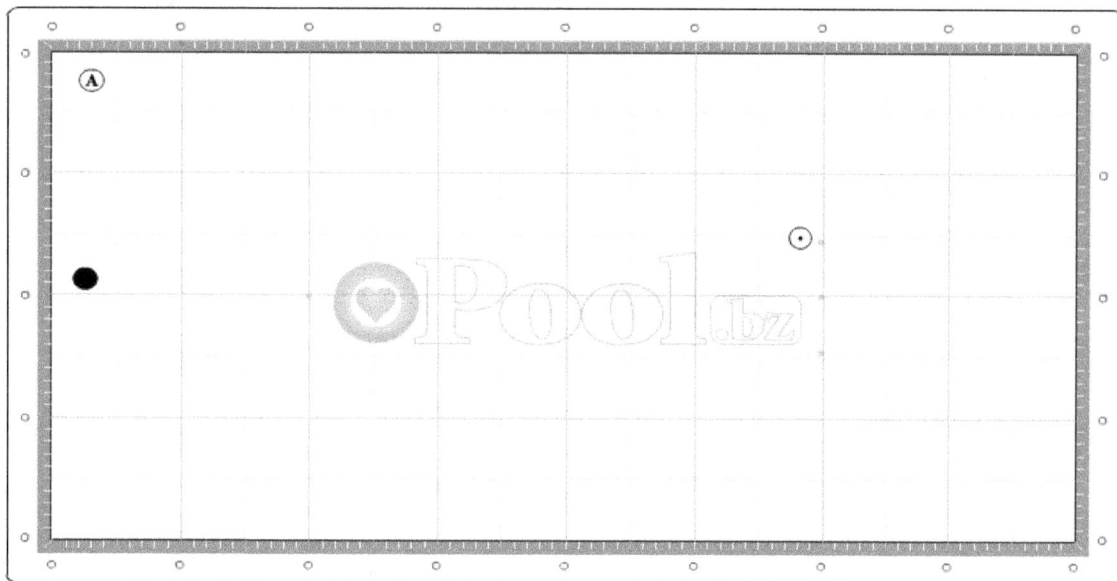

Shot Pattern

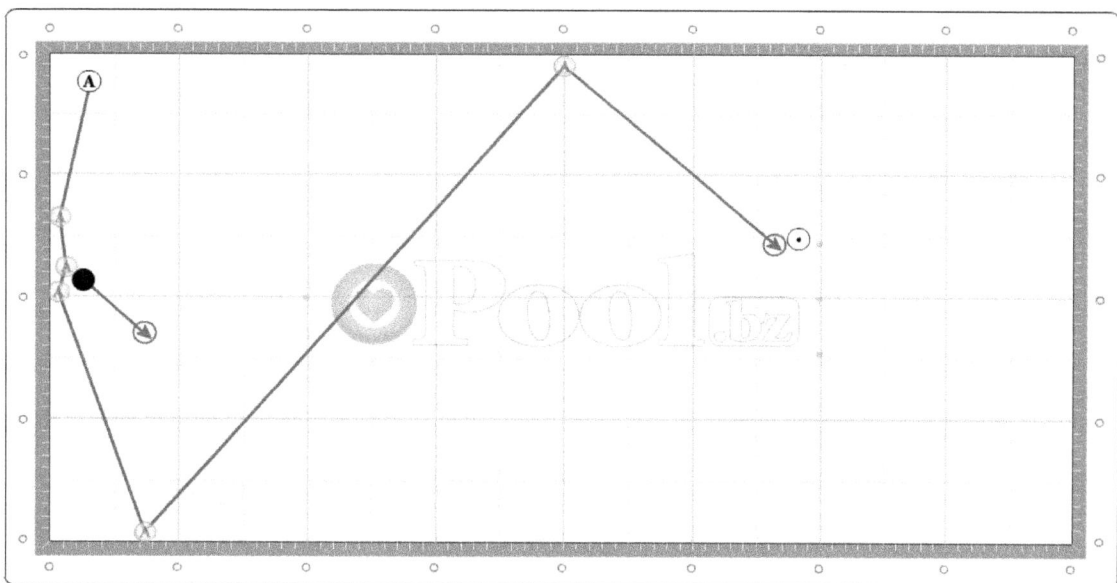

A:1c – Setup

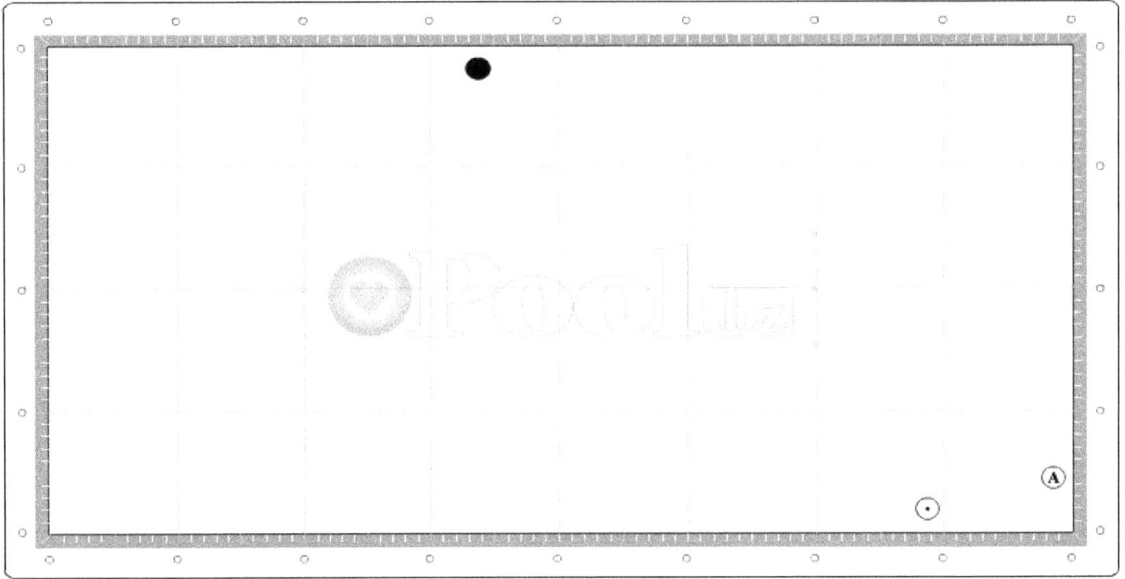

Shot Pattern

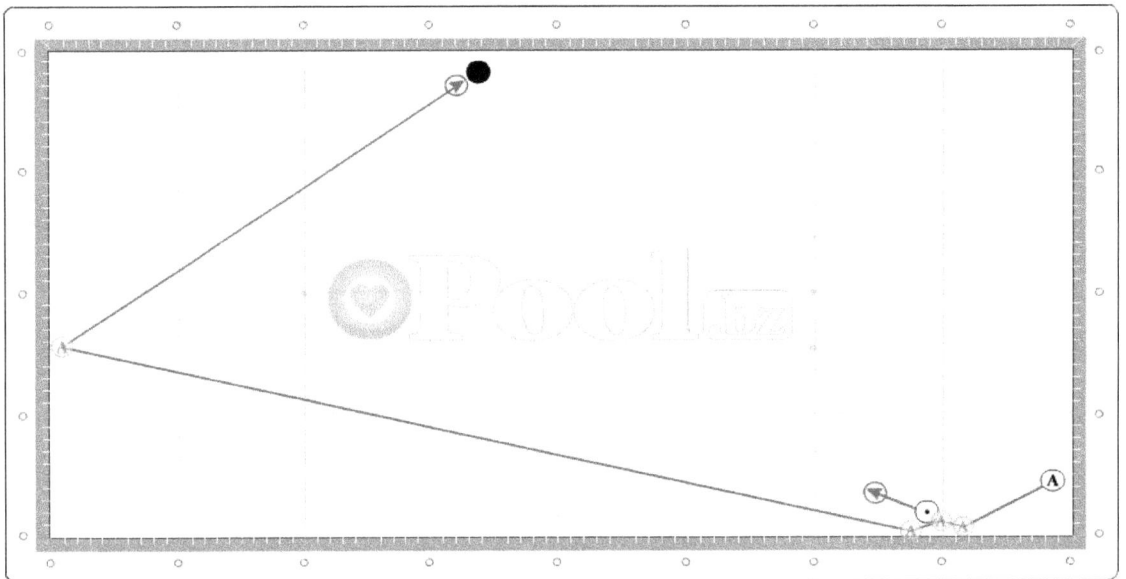

A:1d – Setup

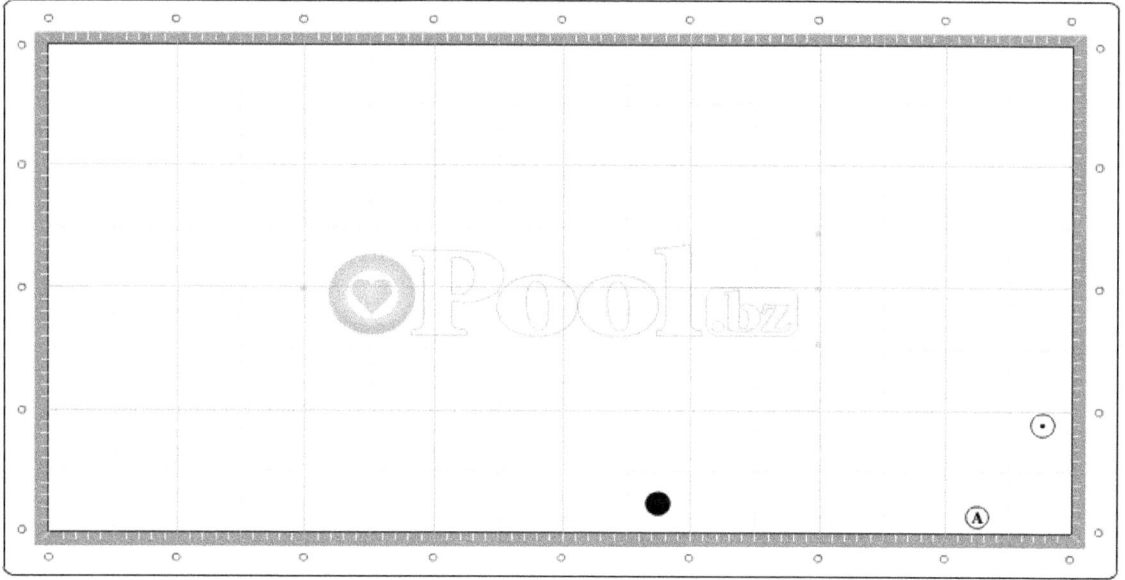

Shot Pattern

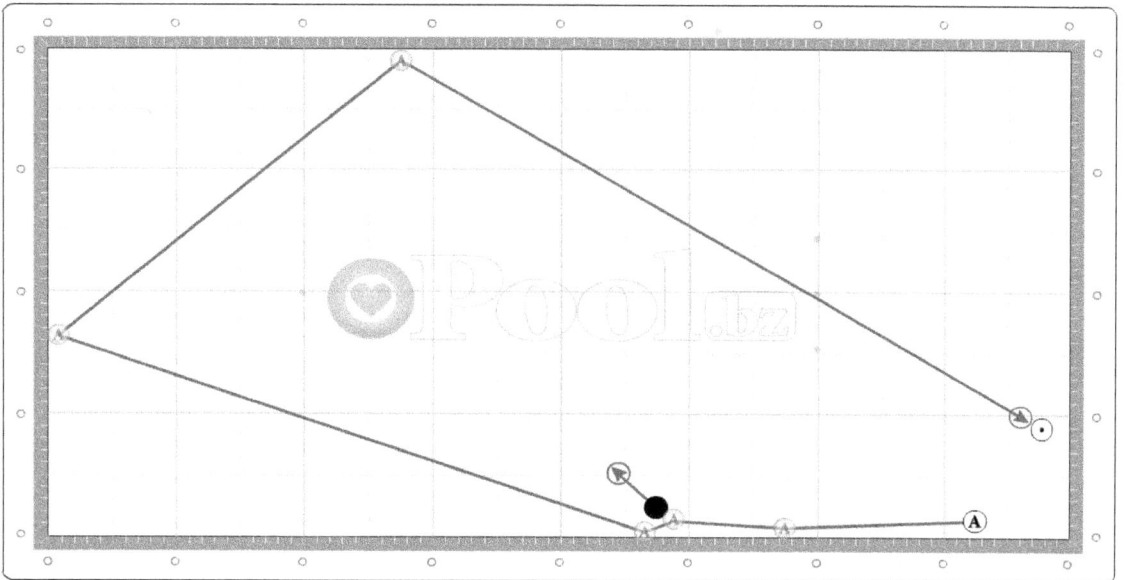

A: Group 2

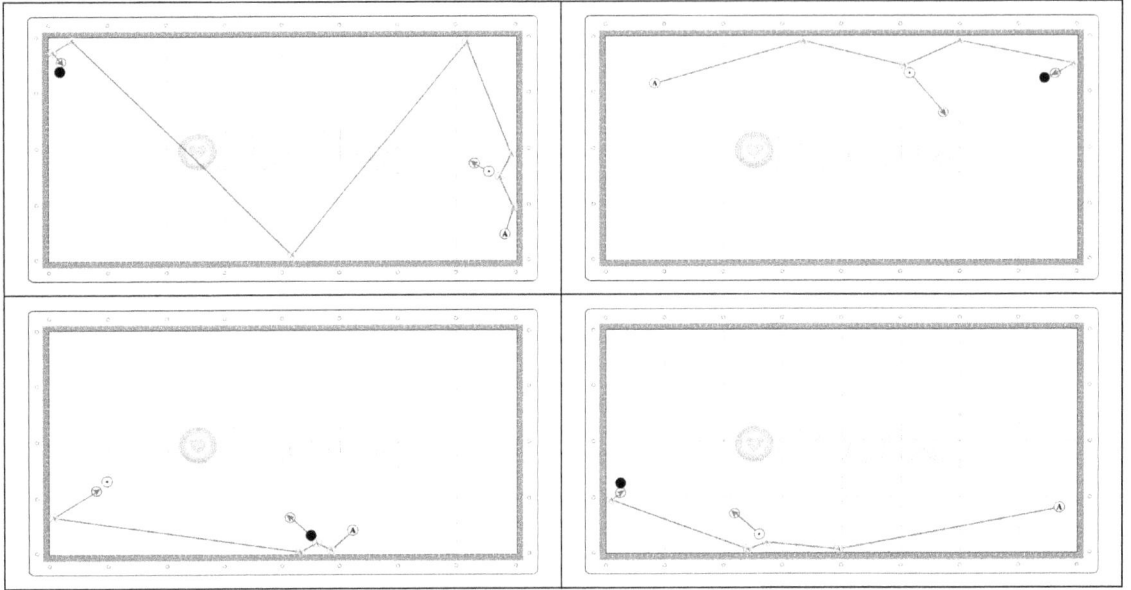

Analysis:

A:2a. _____

A:2b. _____

A:2c. _____

A:2d. _____

A:2a – Setup

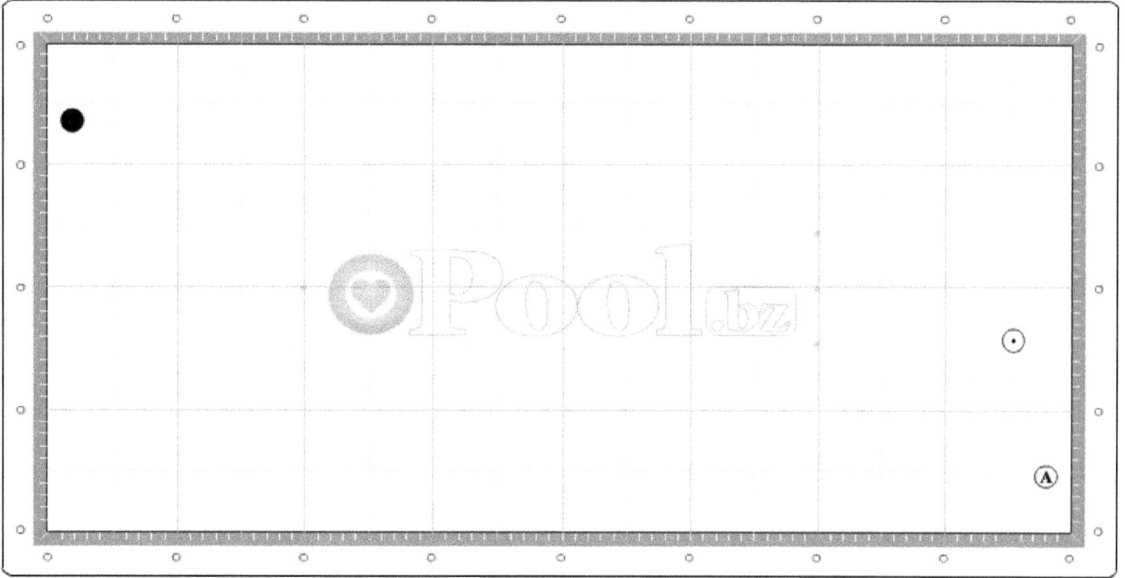

Shot Pattern

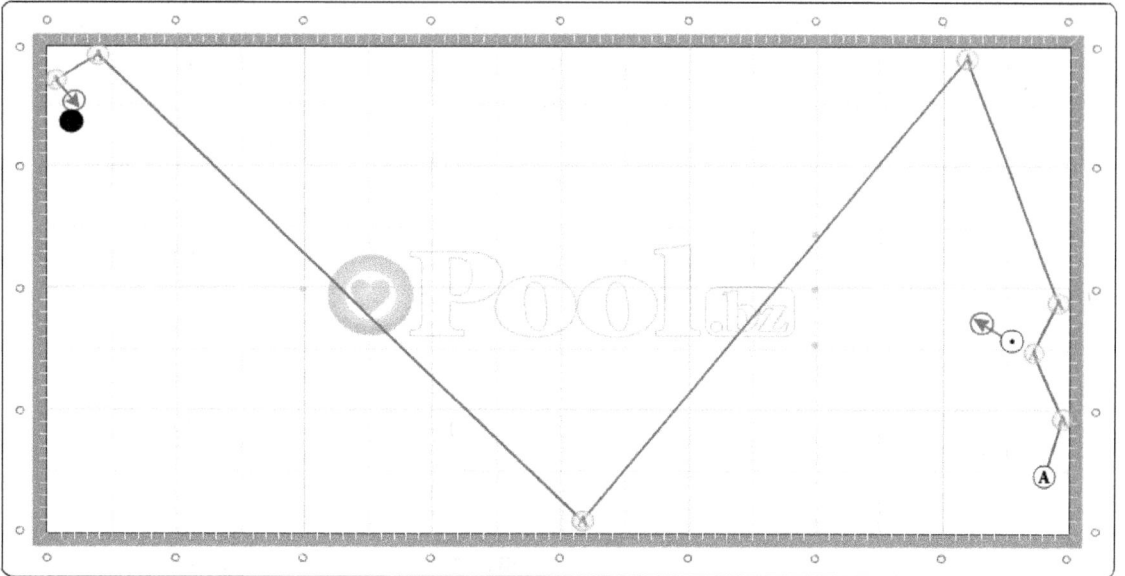

A:2b – Setup

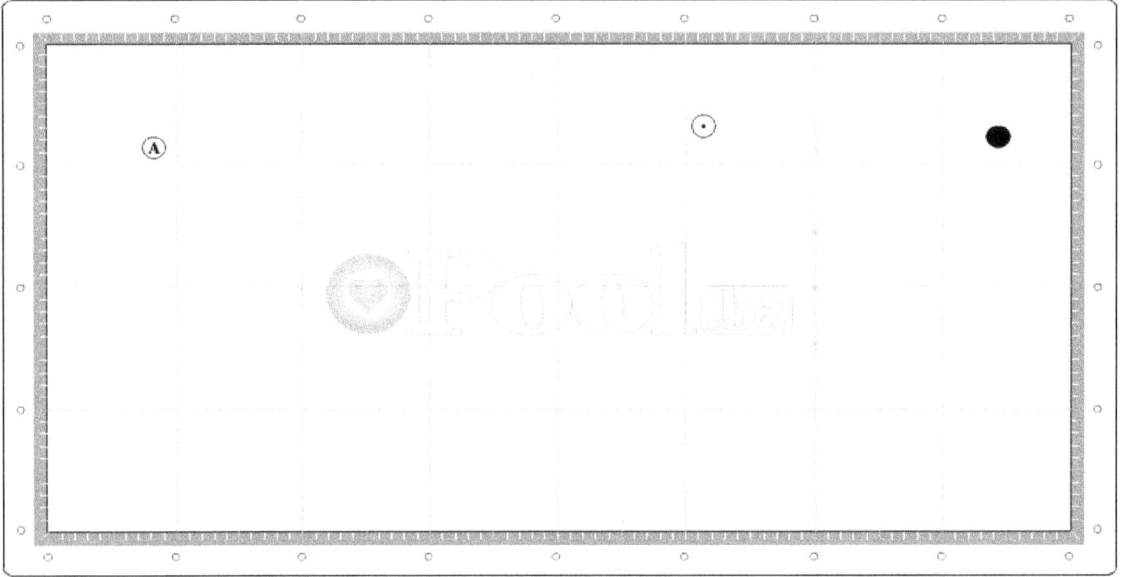

Shot Pattern

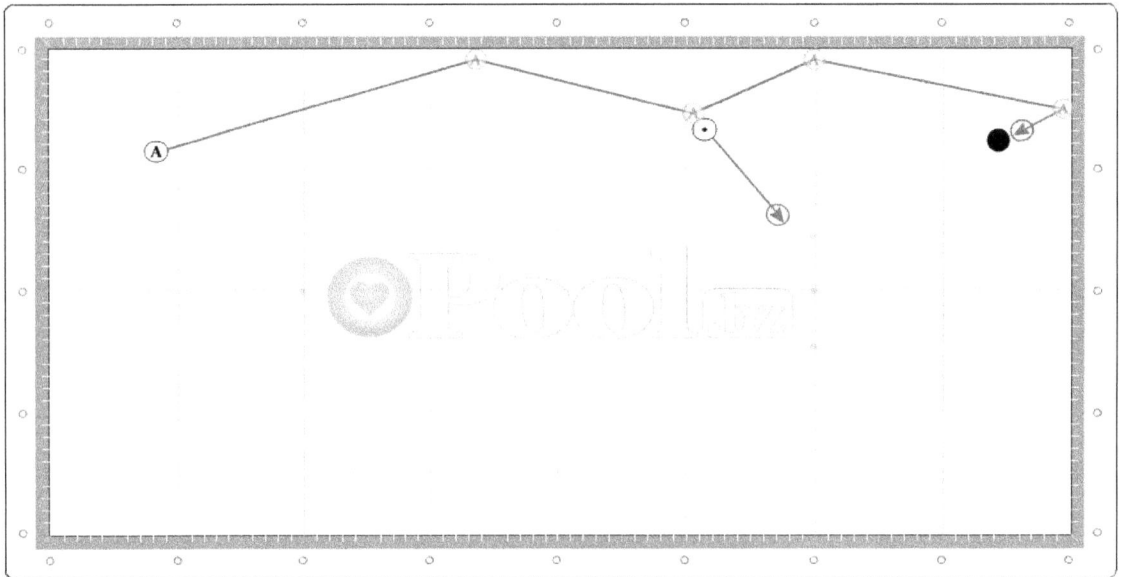

A:2c – Setup

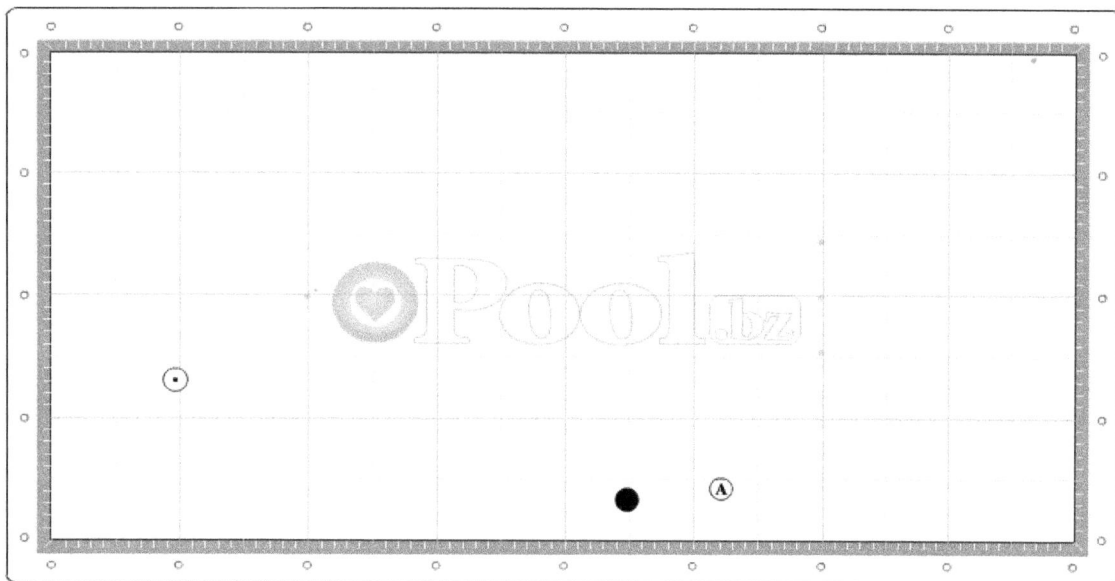

Shot Pattern

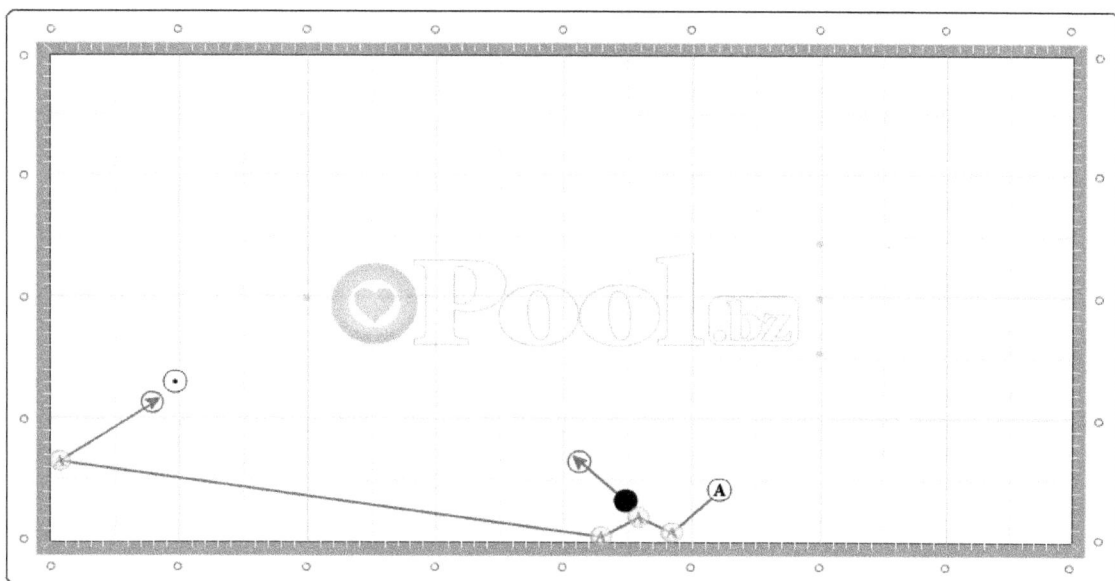

A:2d – Setup

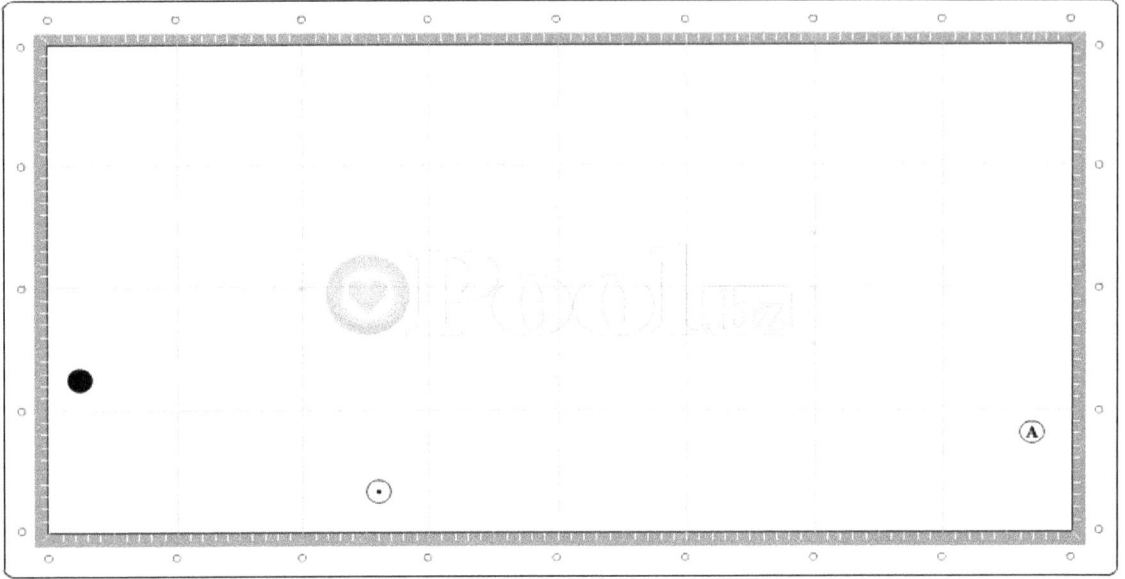

Shot Pattern

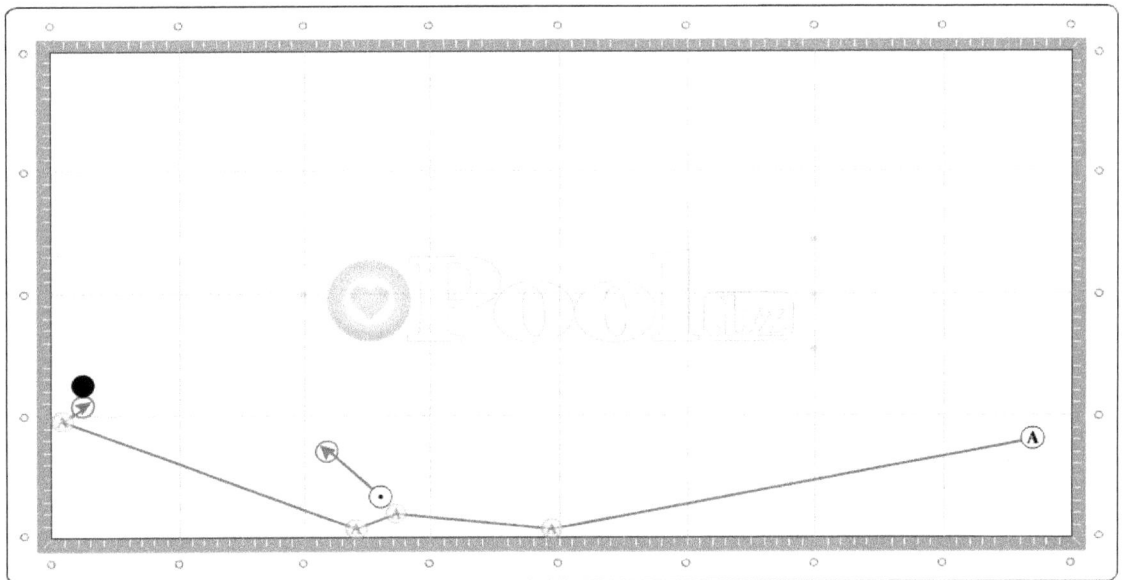

A: Group 3

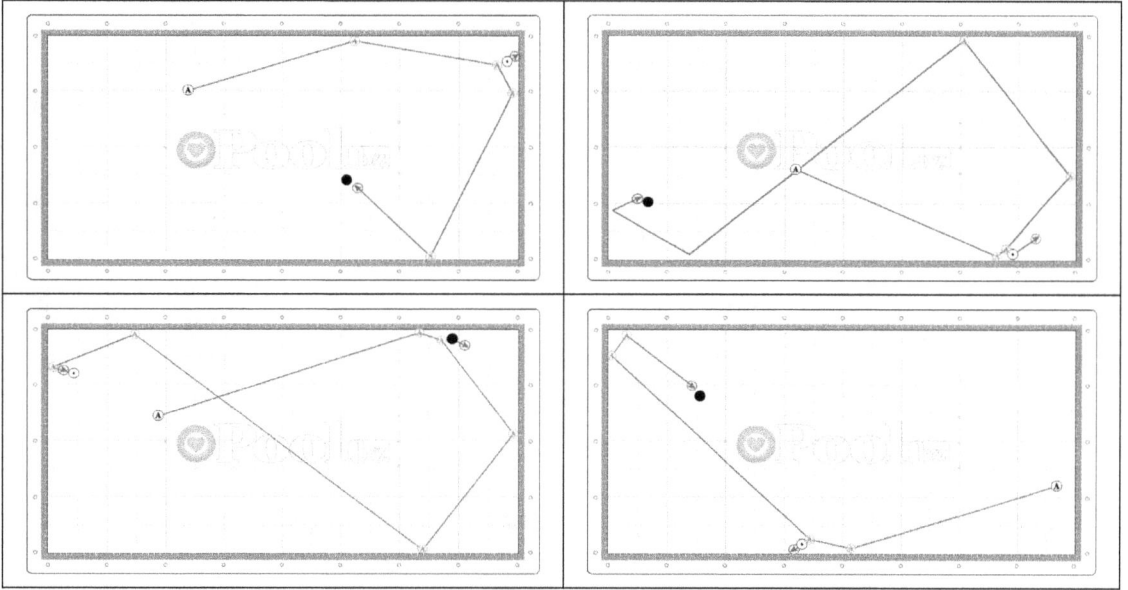

Analysis:

A:3a. _____

A:3b. _____

A:3c. _____

A:3d. _____

A:3a – Setup

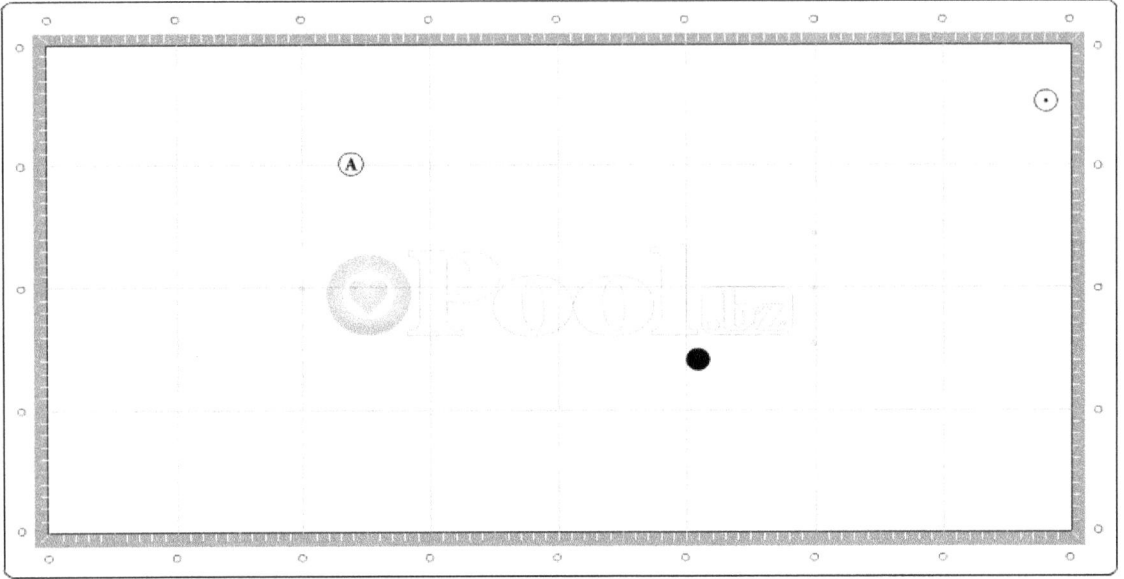

Shot Pattern

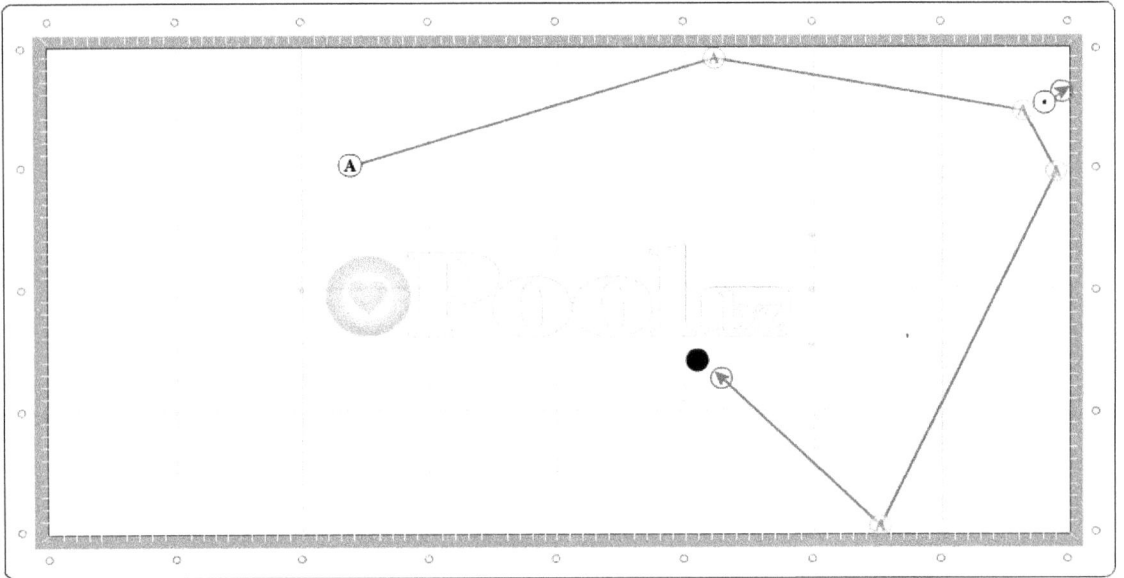

A:3b – Setup

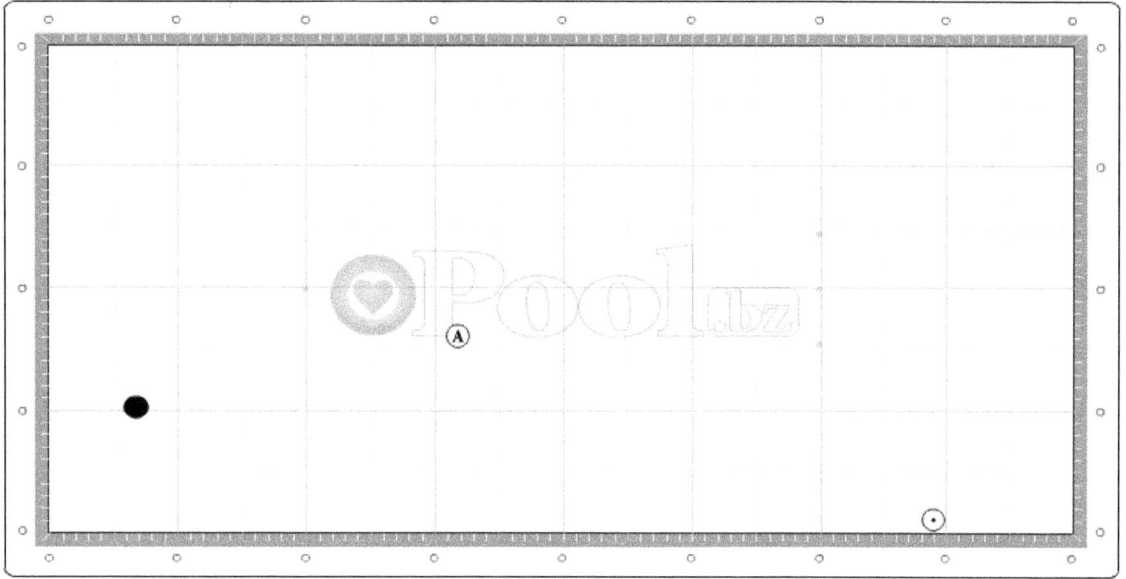

Shot Pattern

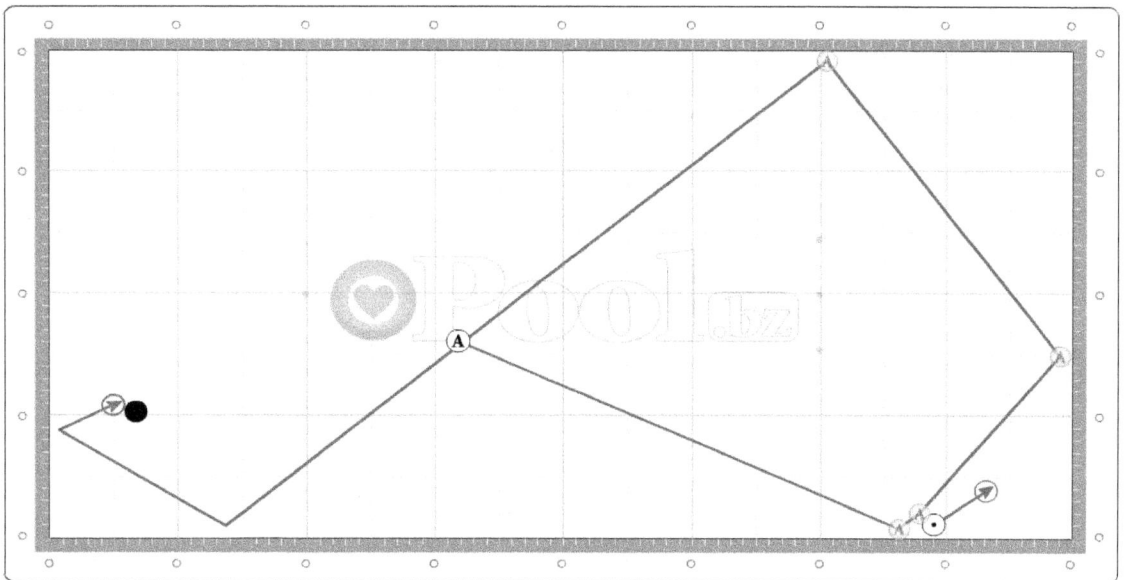

A:3c – Setup

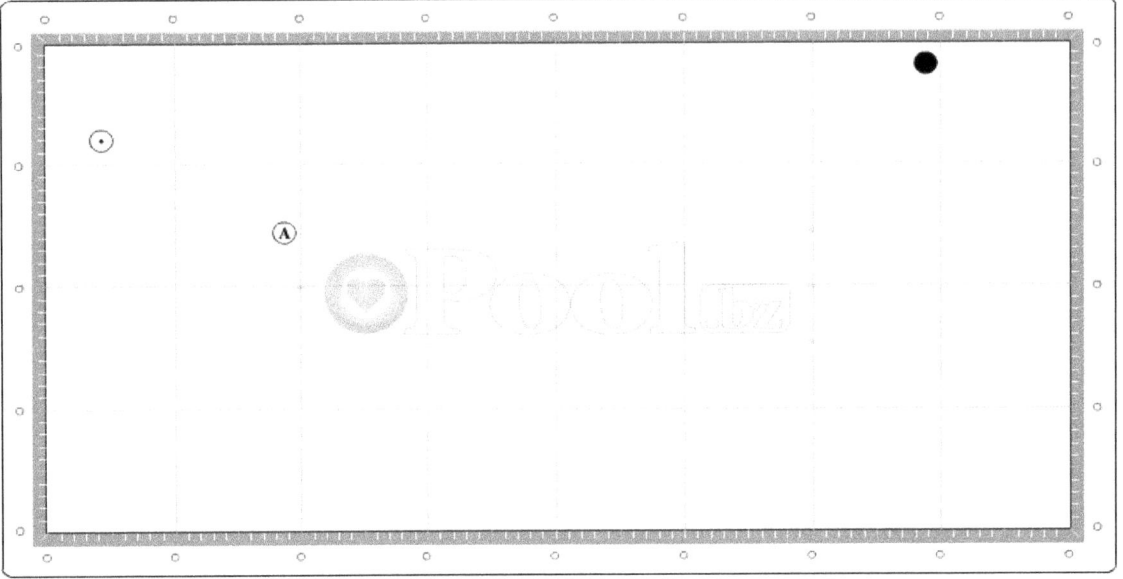

Shot Pattern

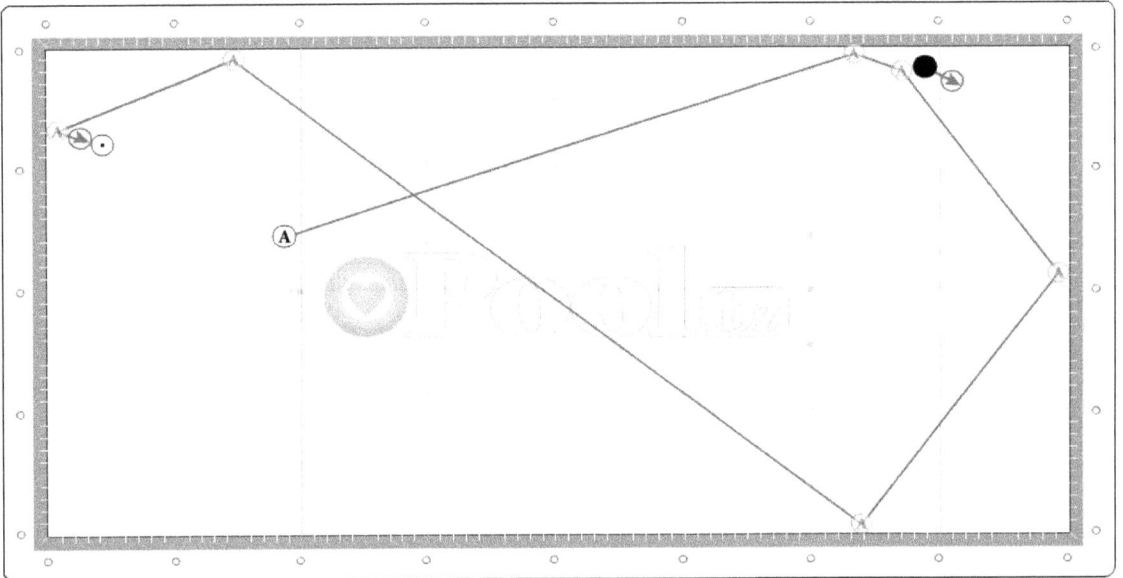

A:3d – Setup

Shot Pattern

A: Group 4

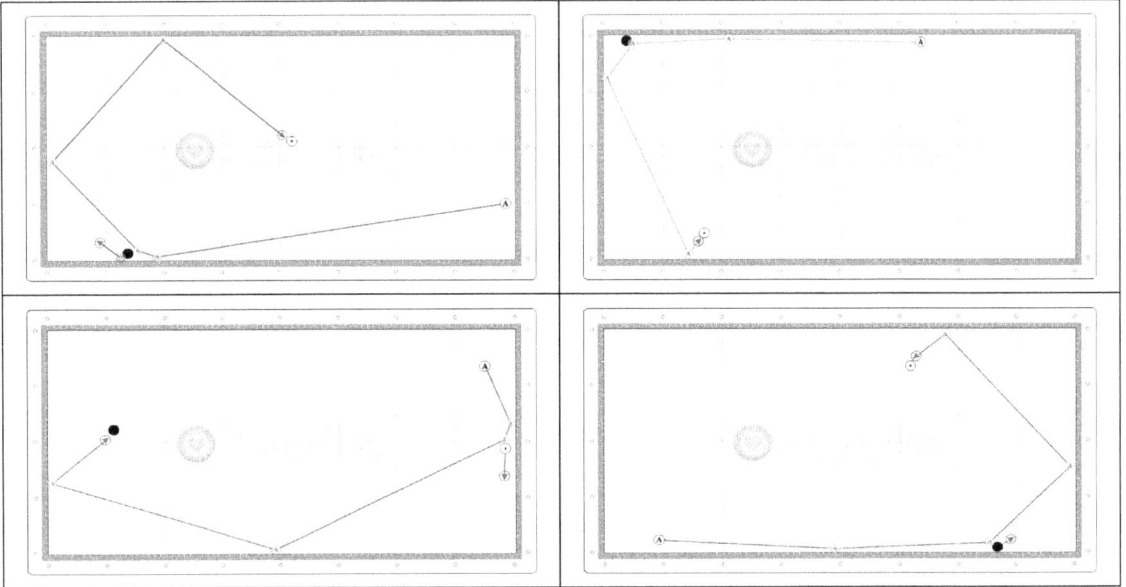

Analysis:

A:4a. _____

A:4b. _____

A:4c. _____

A:4d. _____

A:4a – Setup

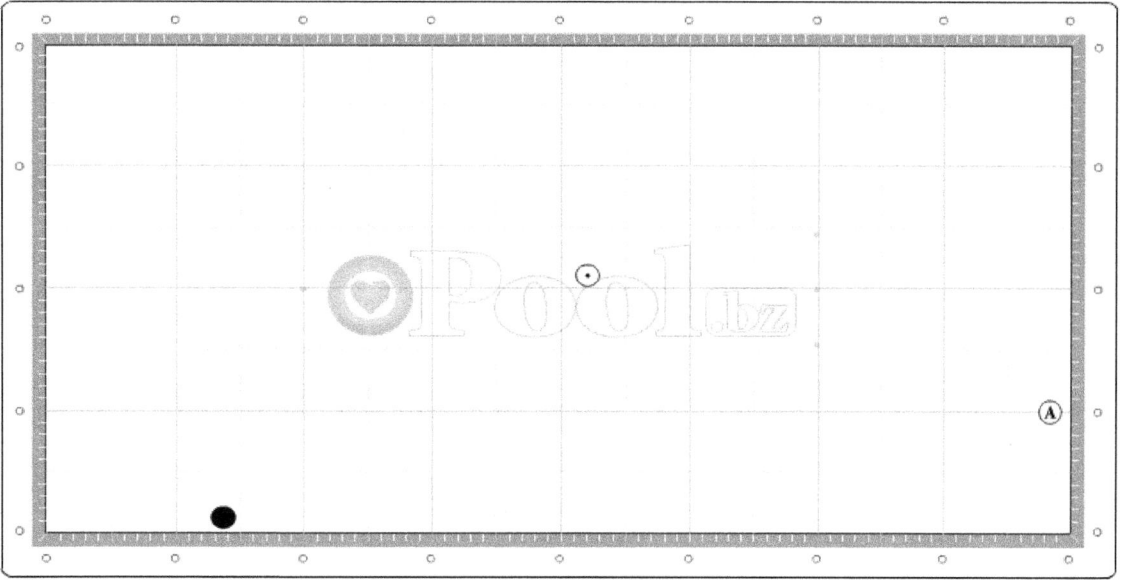

Shot Pattern

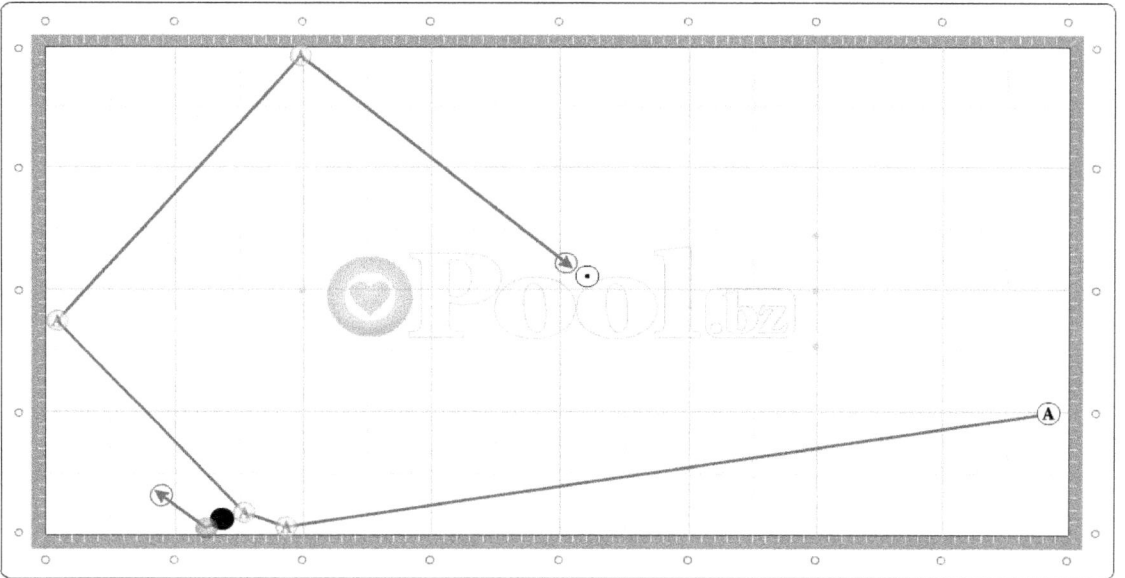

A:4b – Setup

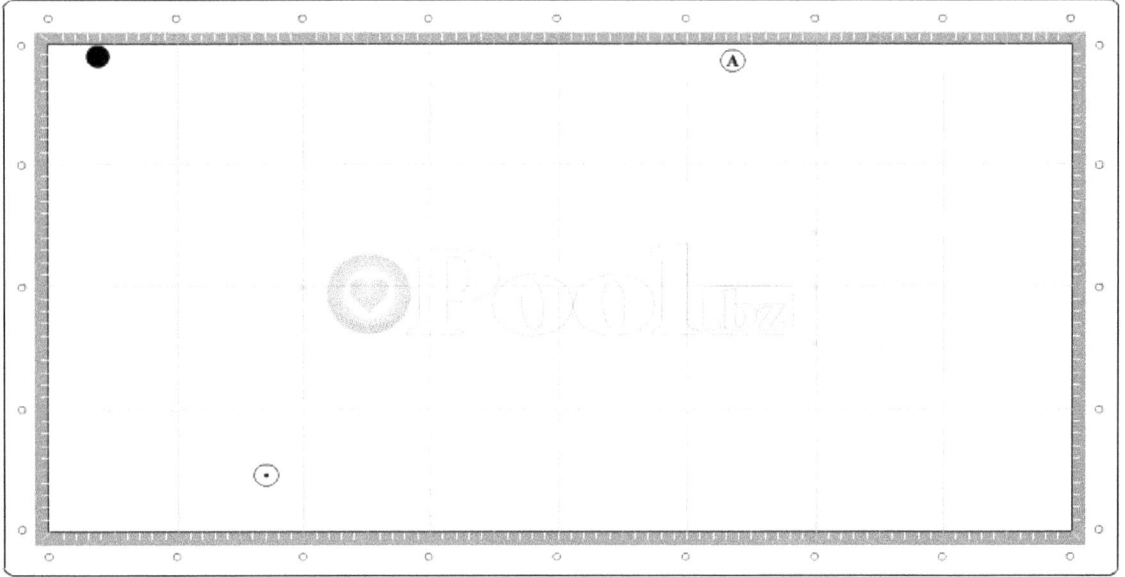

Shot Pattern

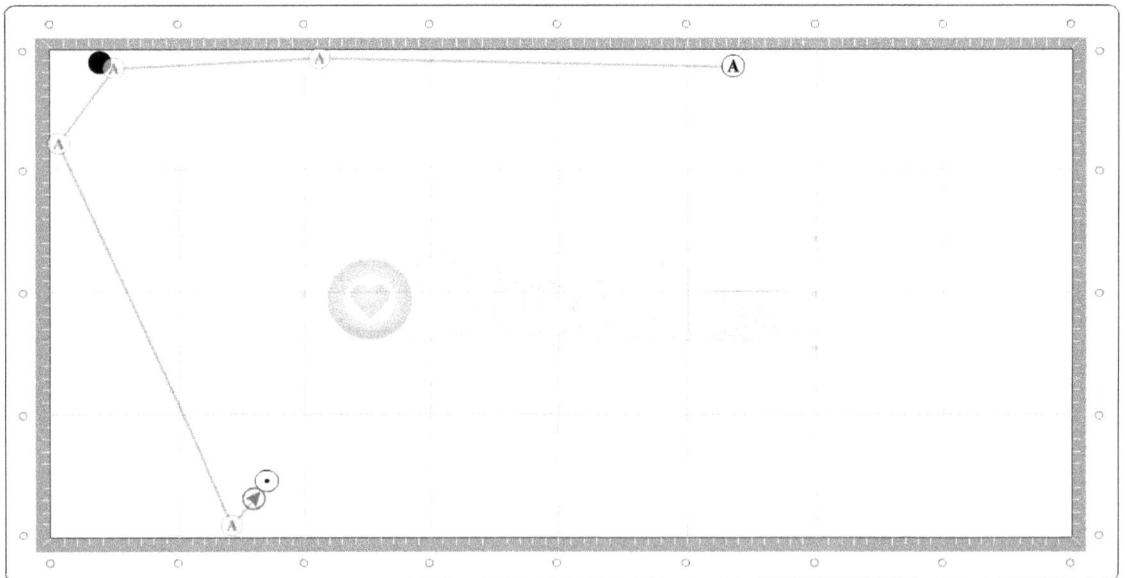

A:4c – Setup

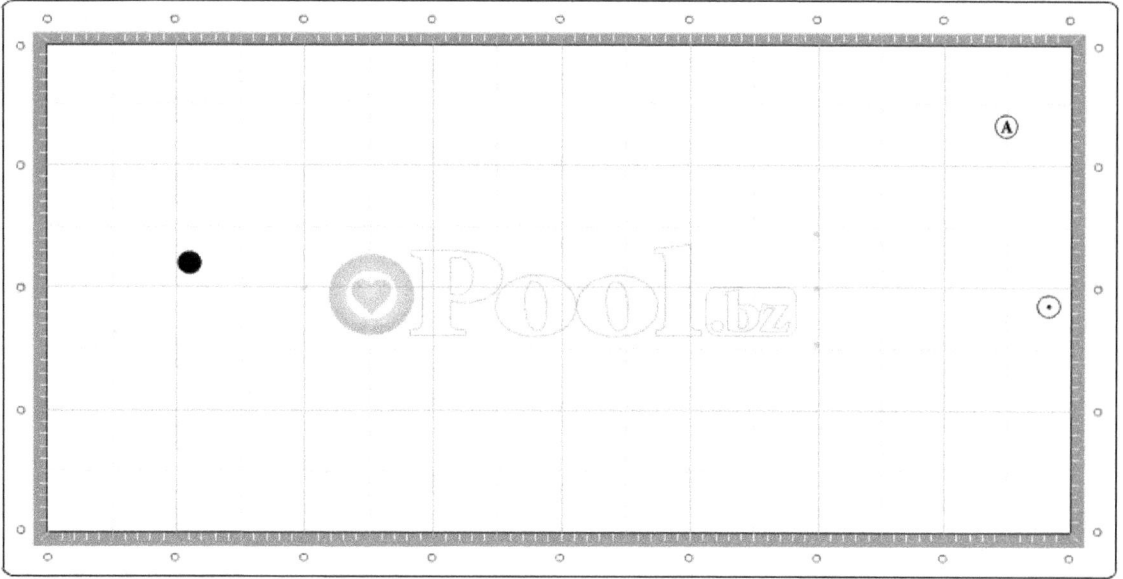

Shot Pattern

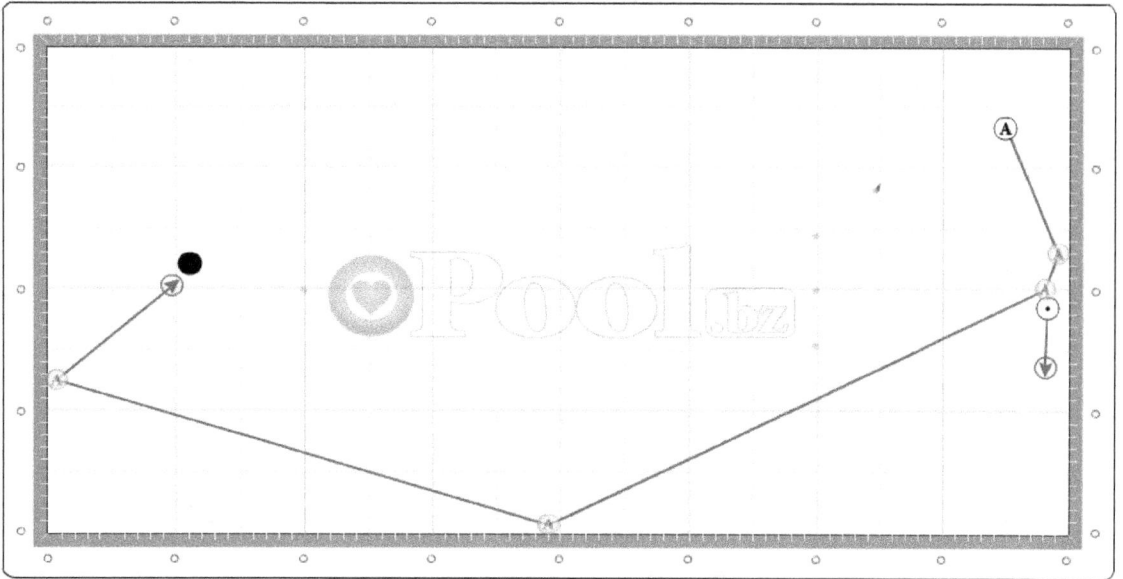

A:4d – Setup

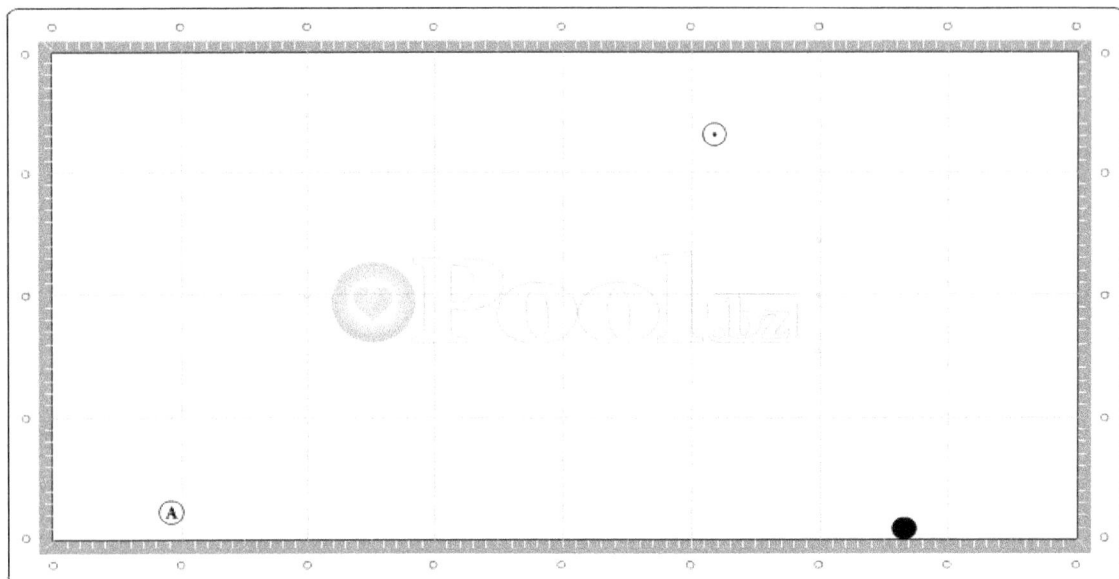

Shot Pattern

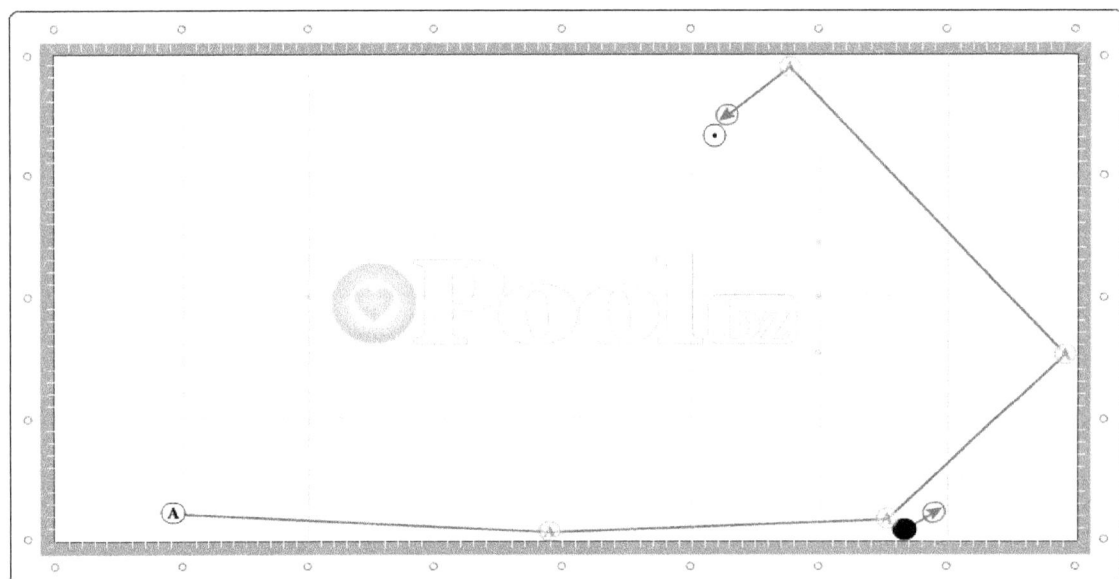

B: 1-rail into a Corner

On these shots, the CB contacts one rail first, then contacts the first OB. The CB then goes into the corner for two more rails. When the CB comes out of the corner to make contact with the second OB for the score. Corners are very useful for two quick cushions.

B: Group 1

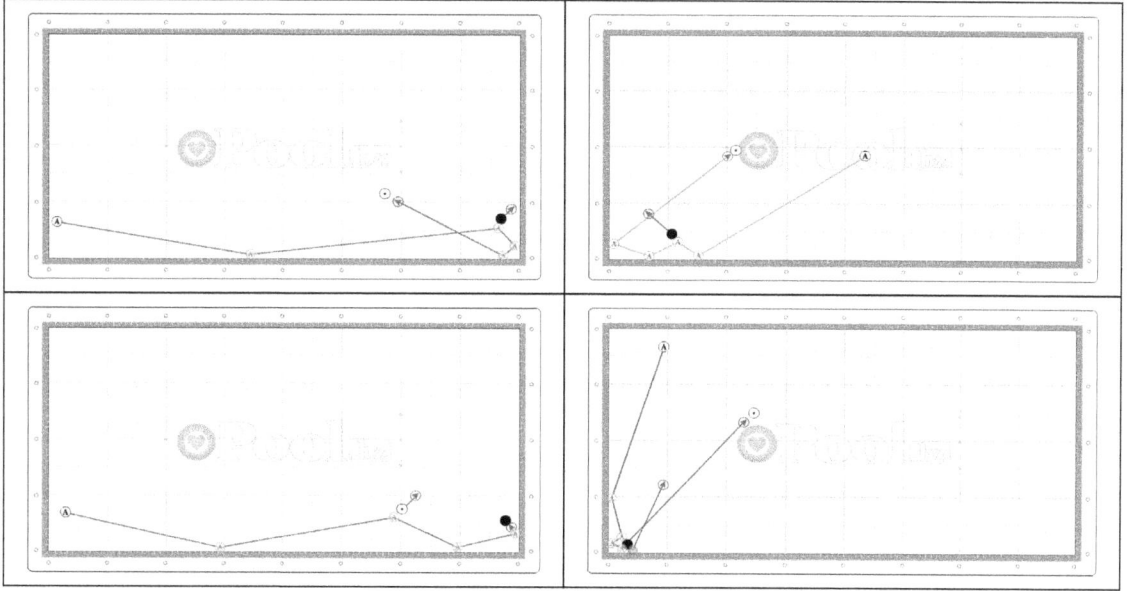

Analysis:

B:1a. _____

B:1b. _____

B:1c. _____

B:1d. _____

B:1a – Setup

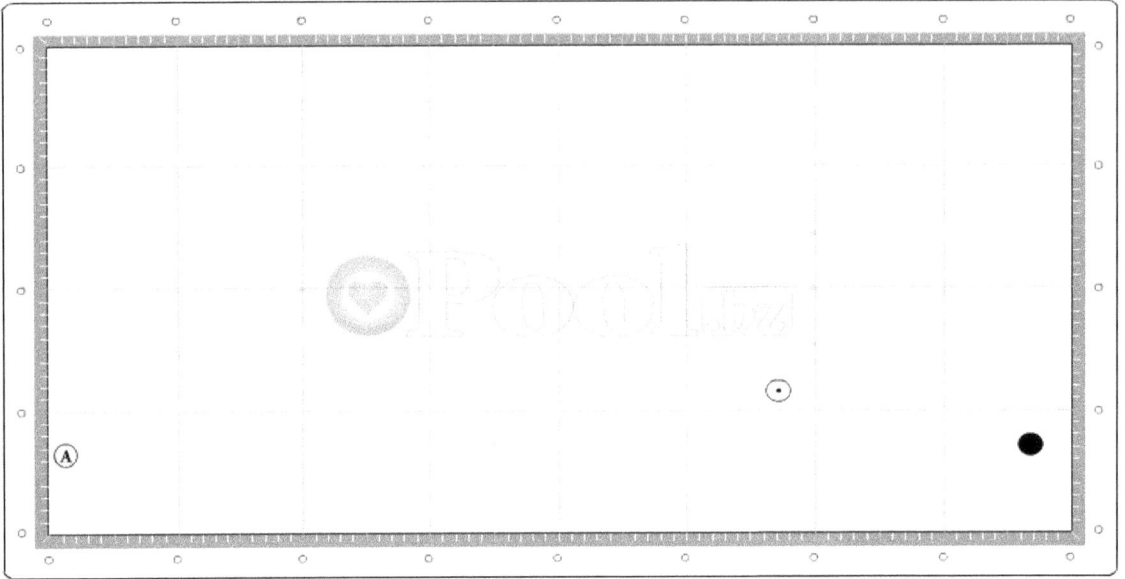

Shot Pattern

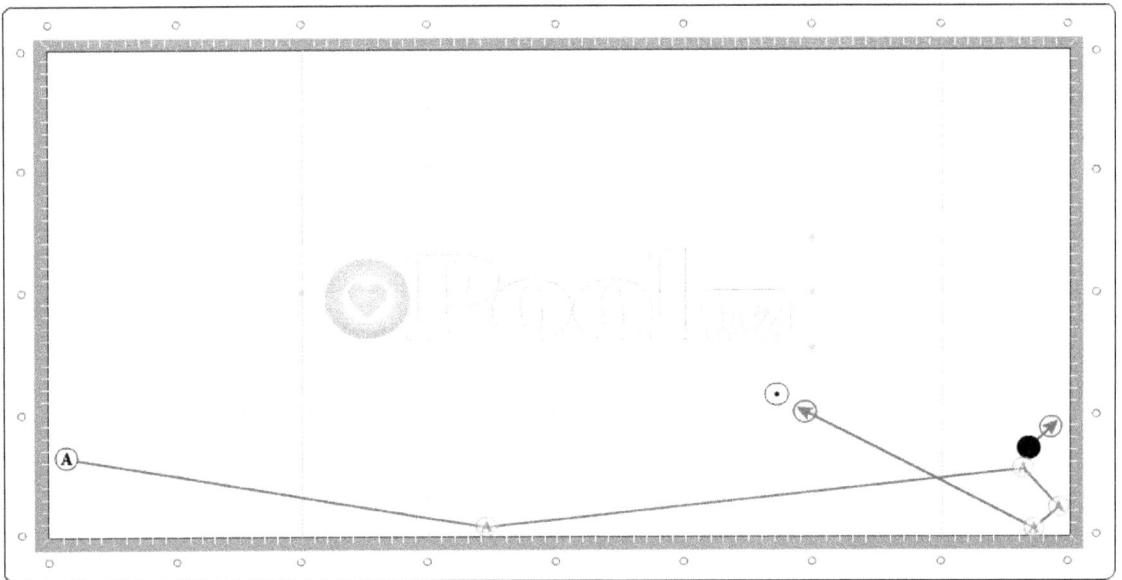

B:1b – Setup

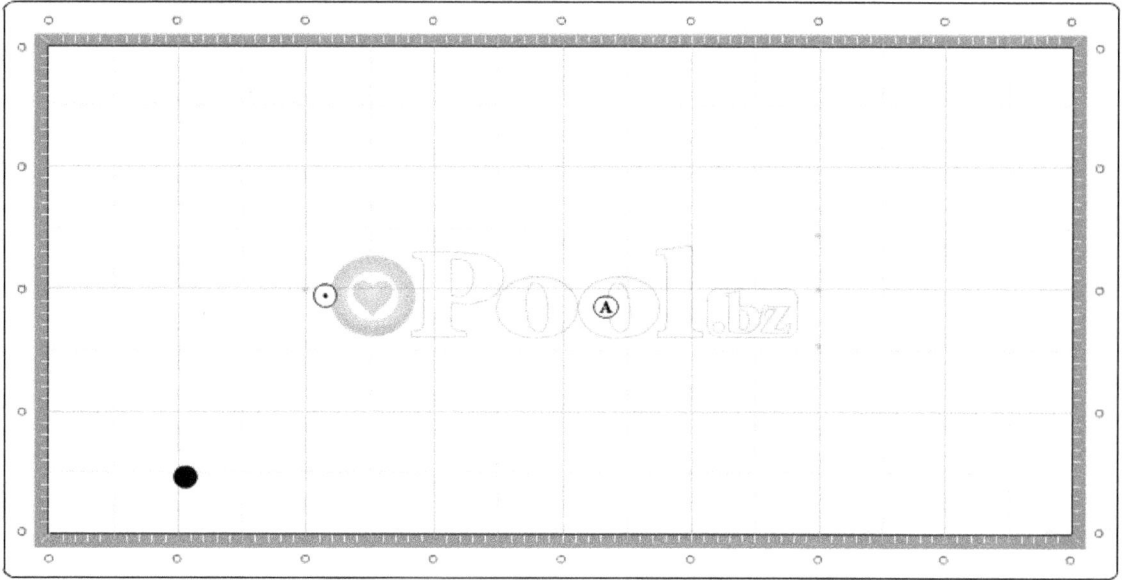

Shot Pattern

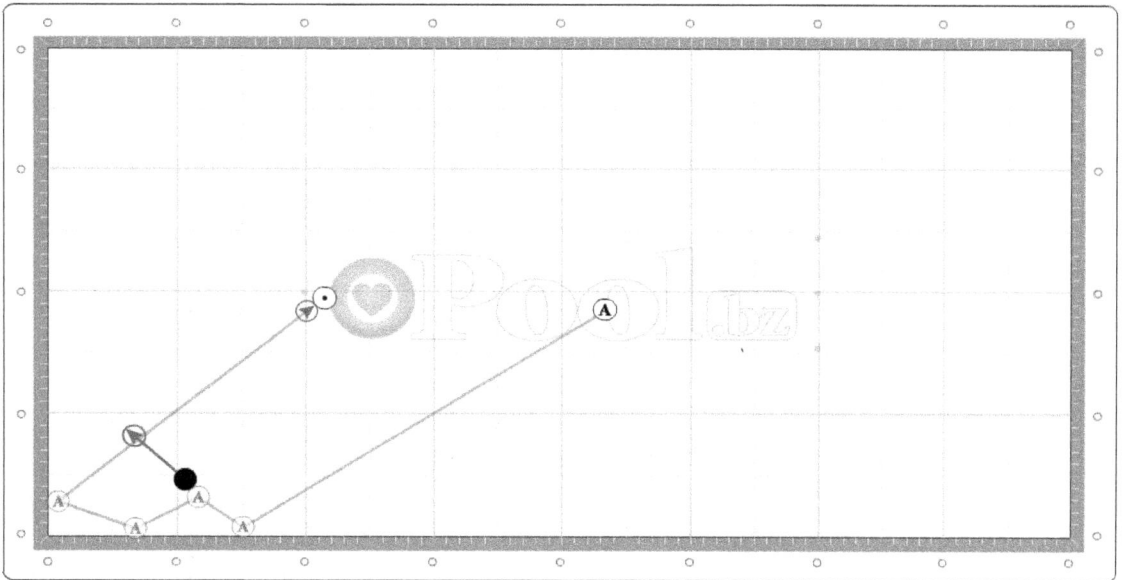

B:1c – Setup

Shot Pattern

B:1d – Setup

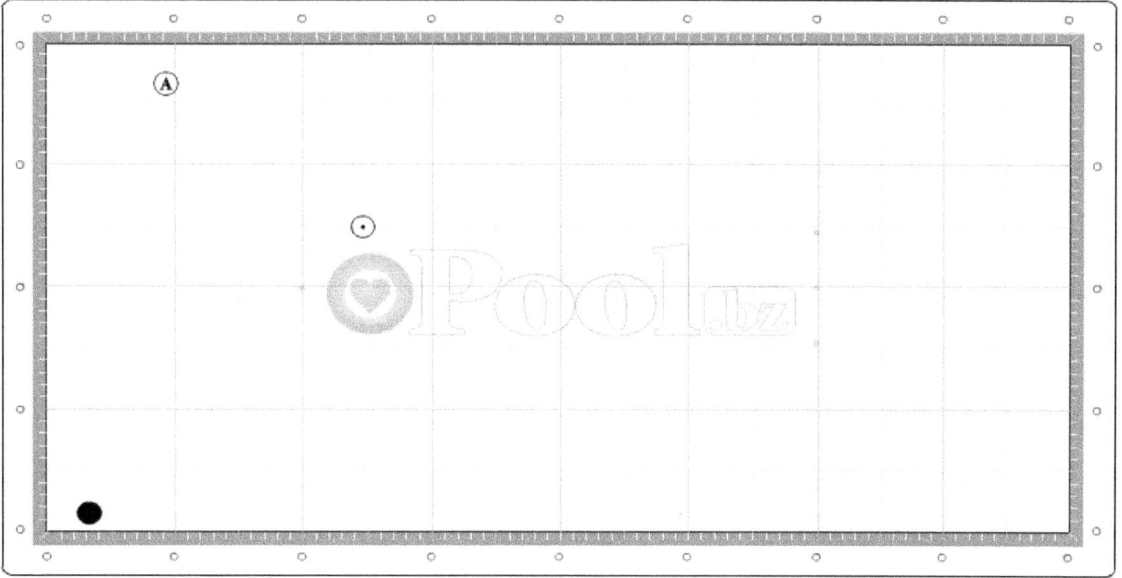

Shot Pattern

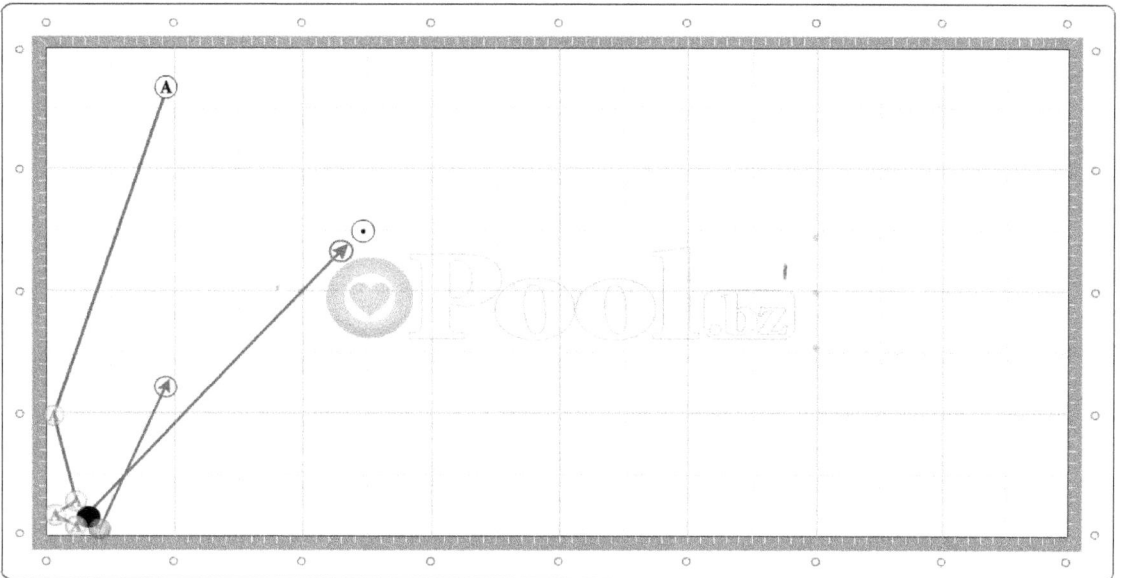

B: Group 2

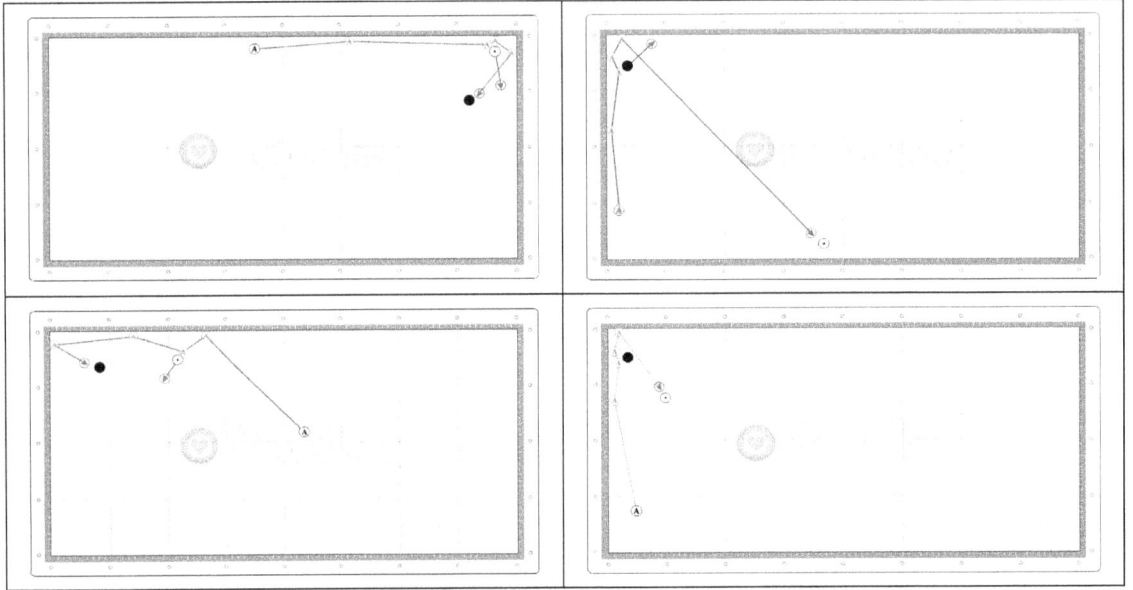

Analysis:

B:2a. _____

B:2b. _____

B:2c. _____

B:2d. _____

B:2a – Setup

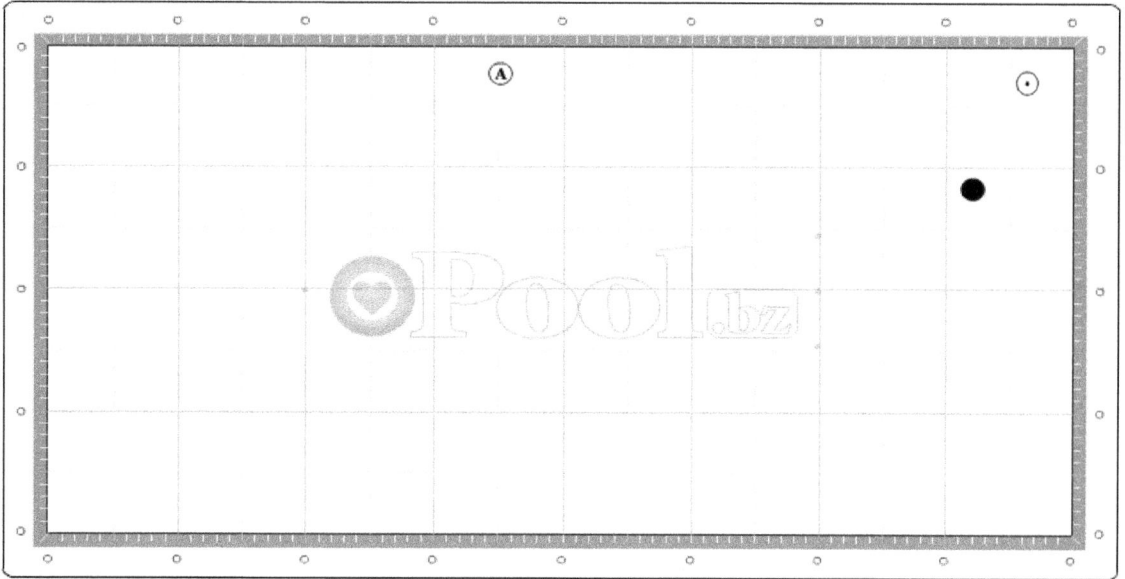

Shot Pattern

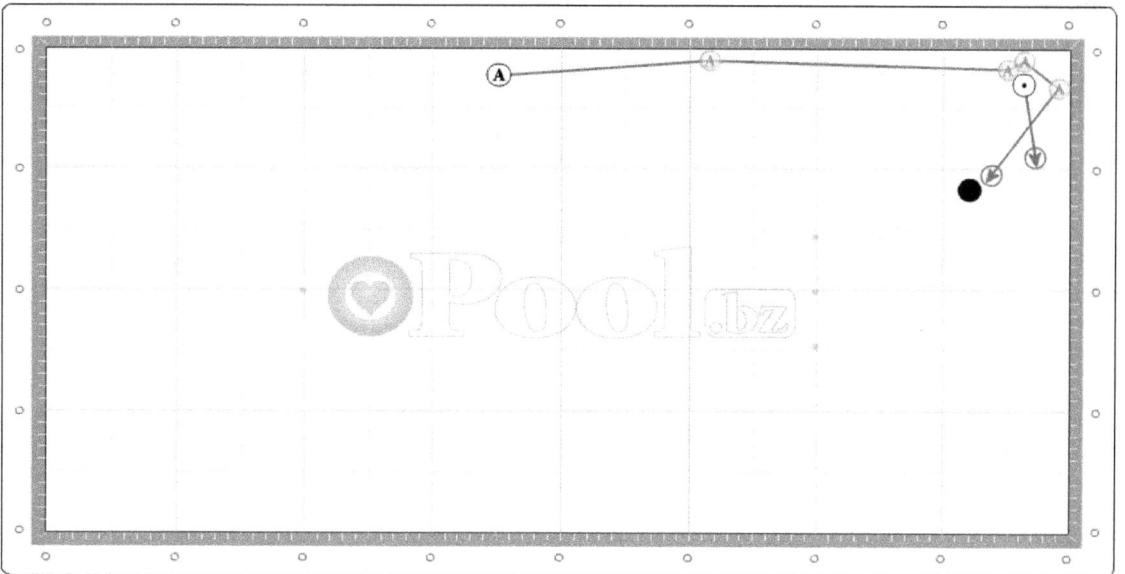

B:2b – Setup

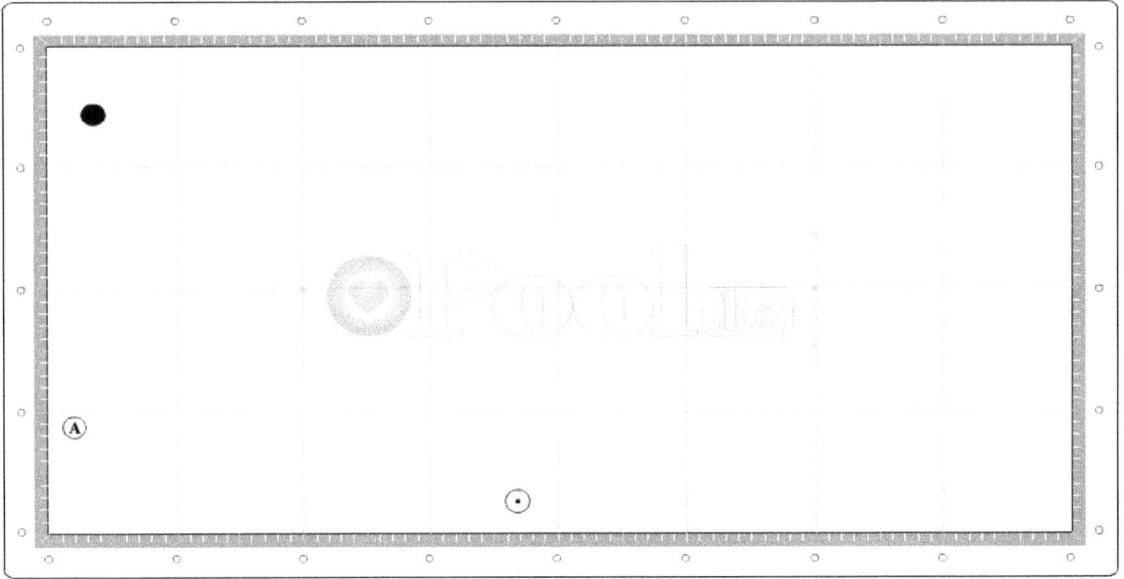

Shot Pattern

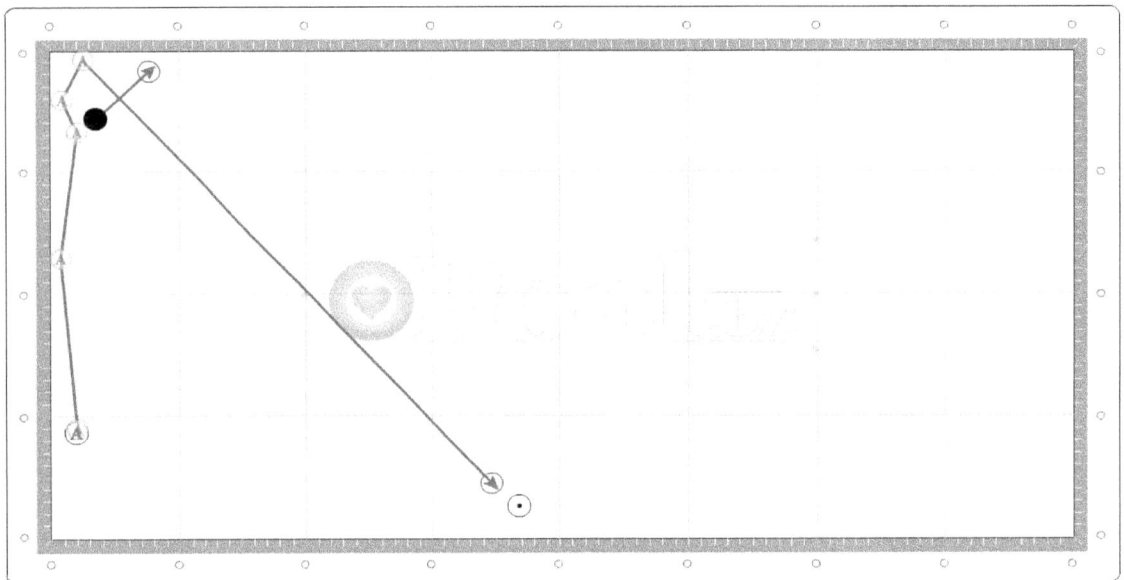

B:2c – Setup

Shot Pattern

B:2d – Setup

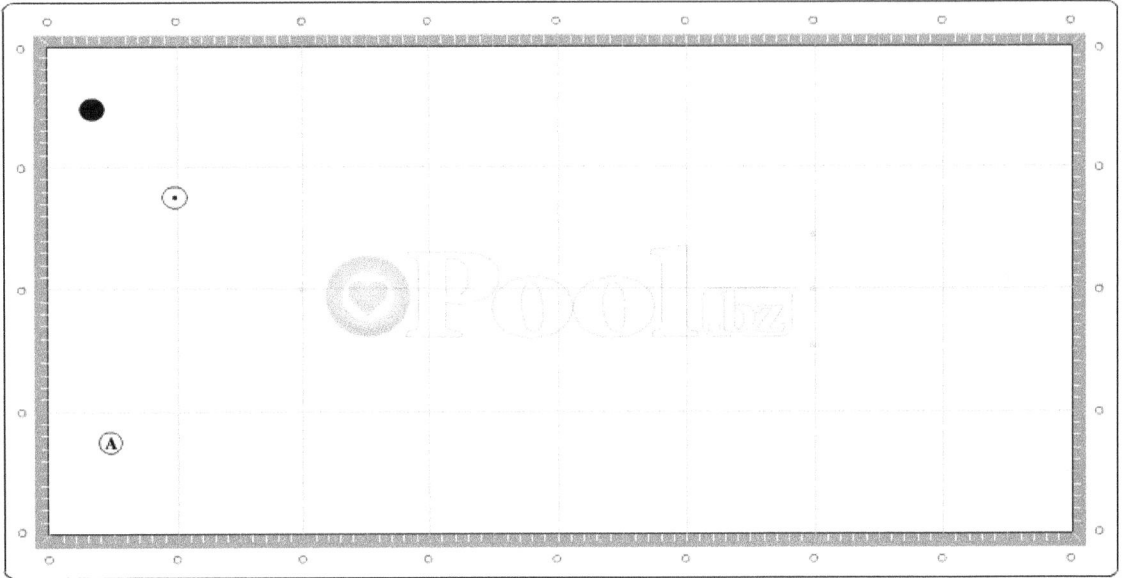

Shot Pattern

C: 2 cushions first

On these shots, the CB goes into two rails before it contacts the first OB. After the contact with the first OB, the CB then goes into another cushion (or more) and then contacting the second OB for the point. These can a lot of fun!

C: Group 1

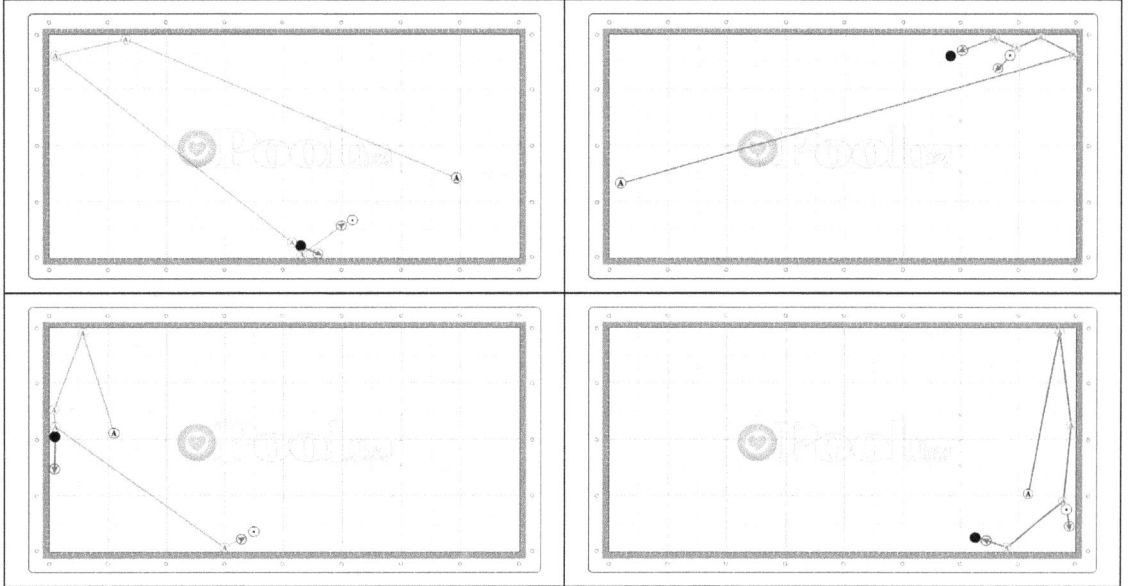

Analysis:

C:1a. _____

C:1b. _____

C:1c. _____

C:1d. _____

C:1a – Setup

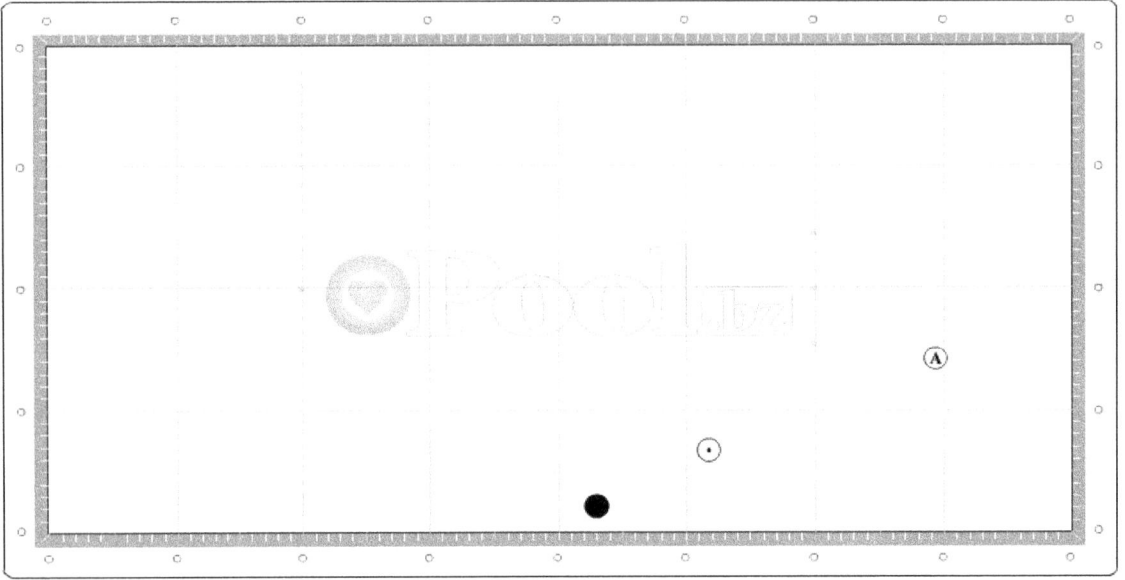

Shot Pattern

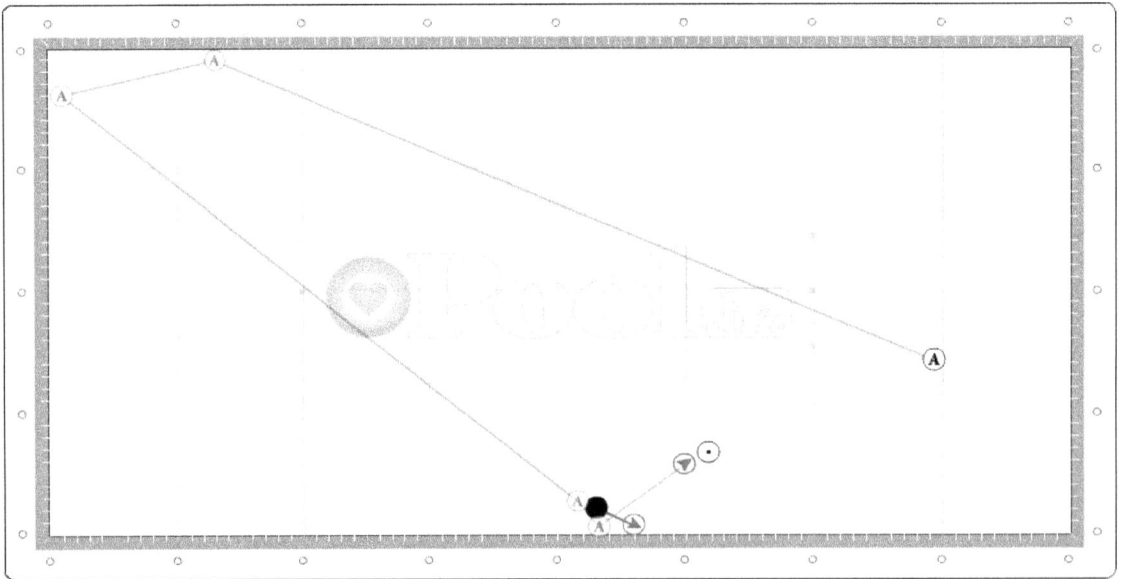

C:1b – Setup

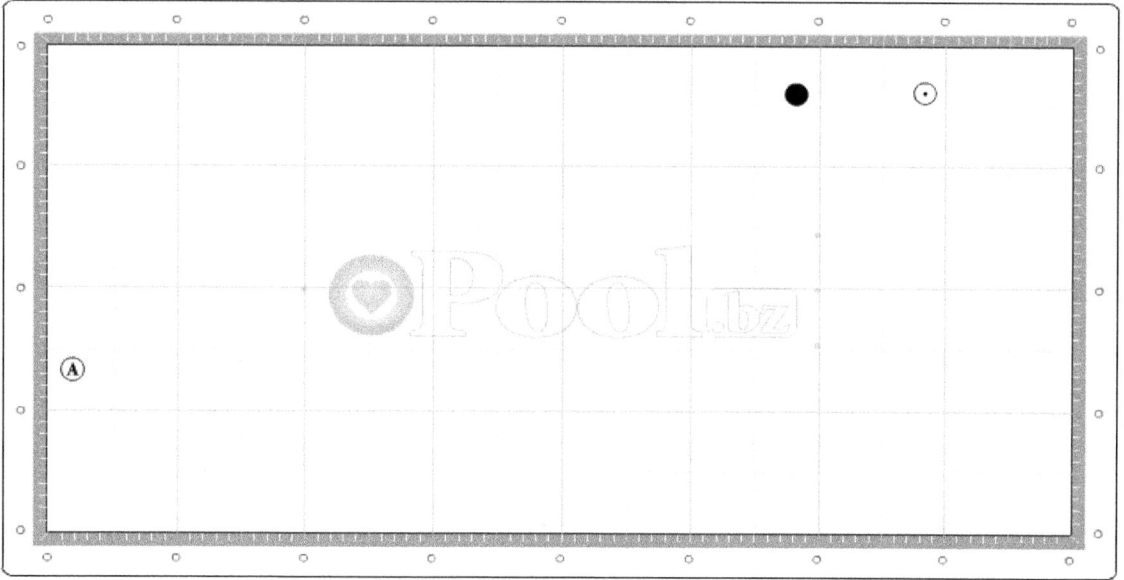

Shot Pattern

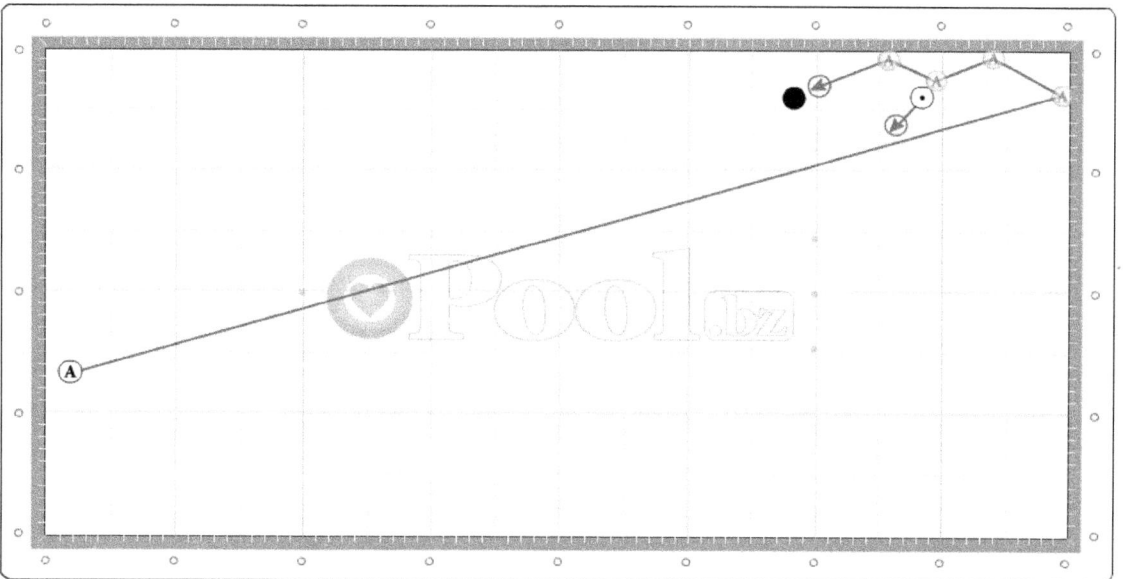

C:1c – Setup

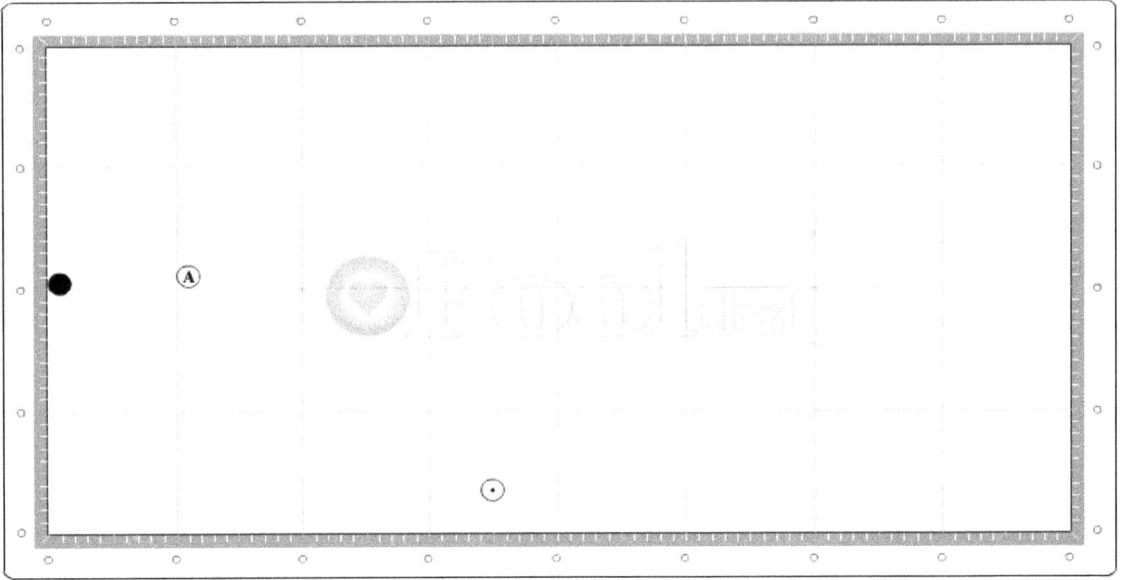

Shot Pattern

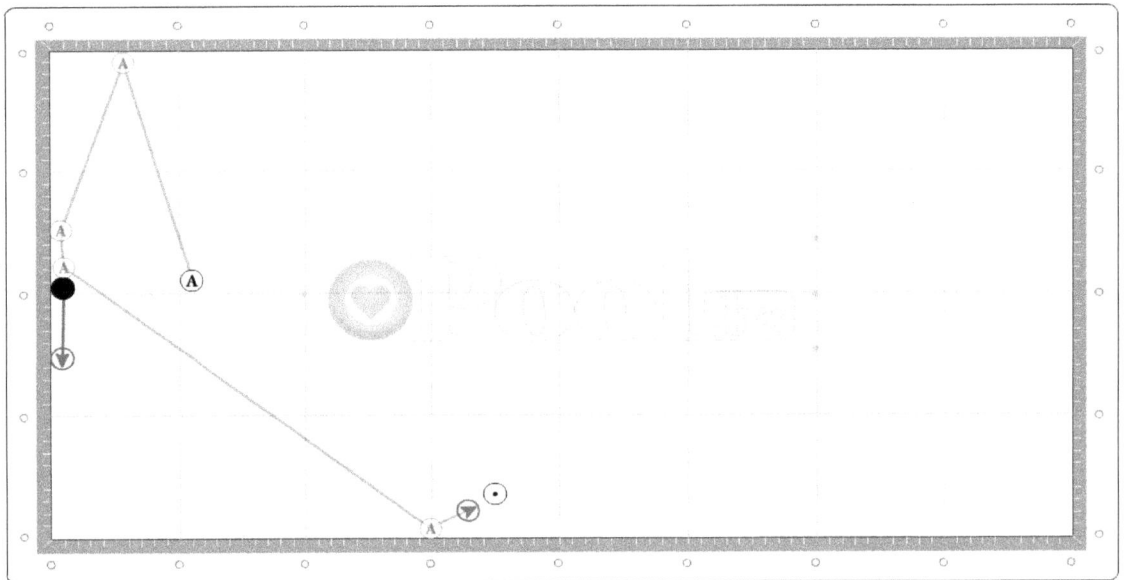

C:1d – Setup

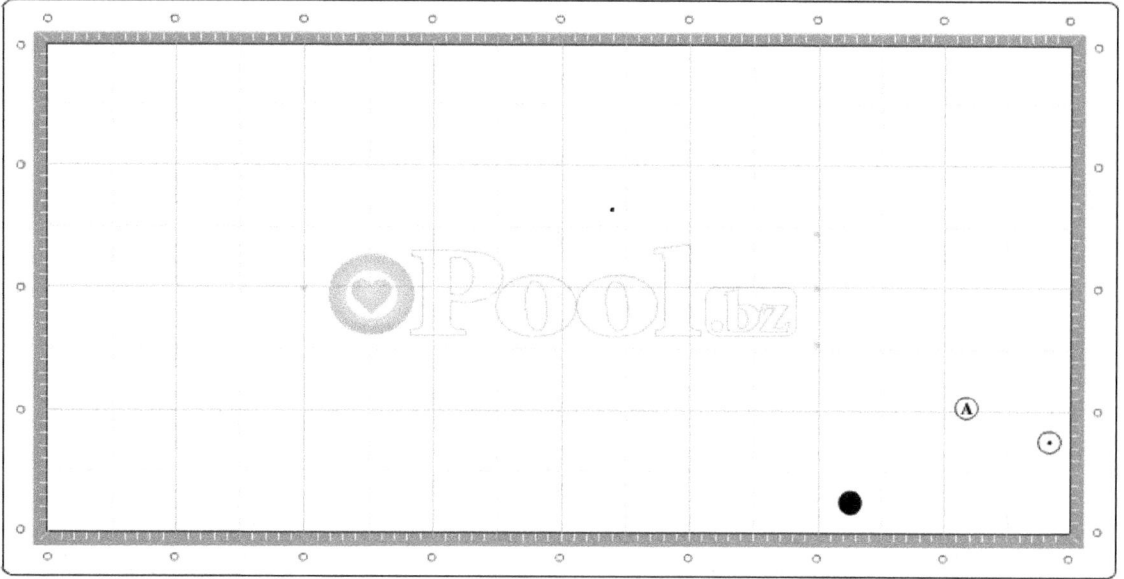

Shot Pattern

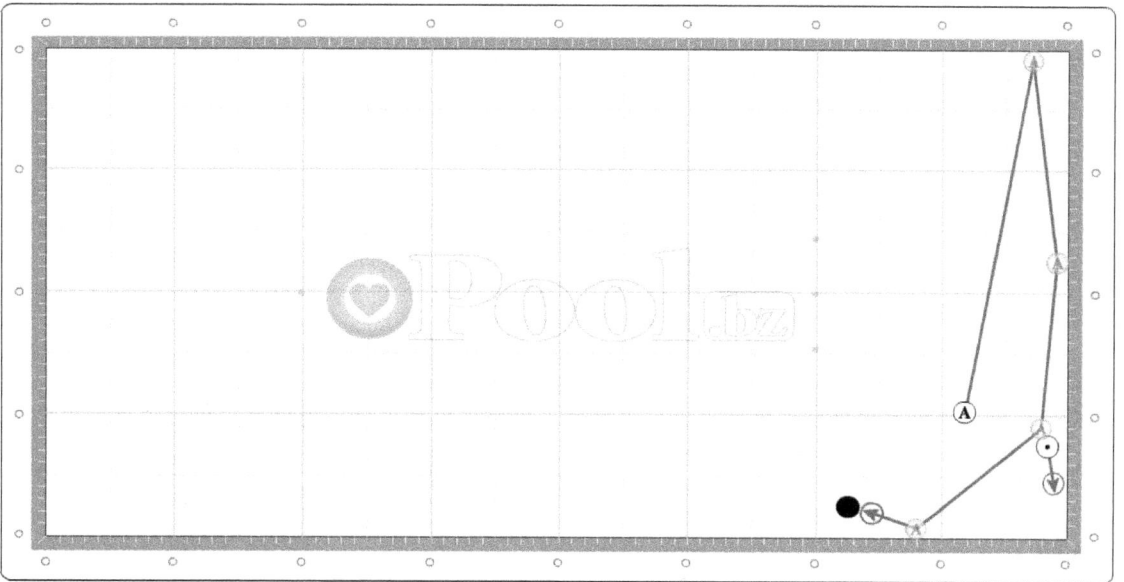

C: Group 2

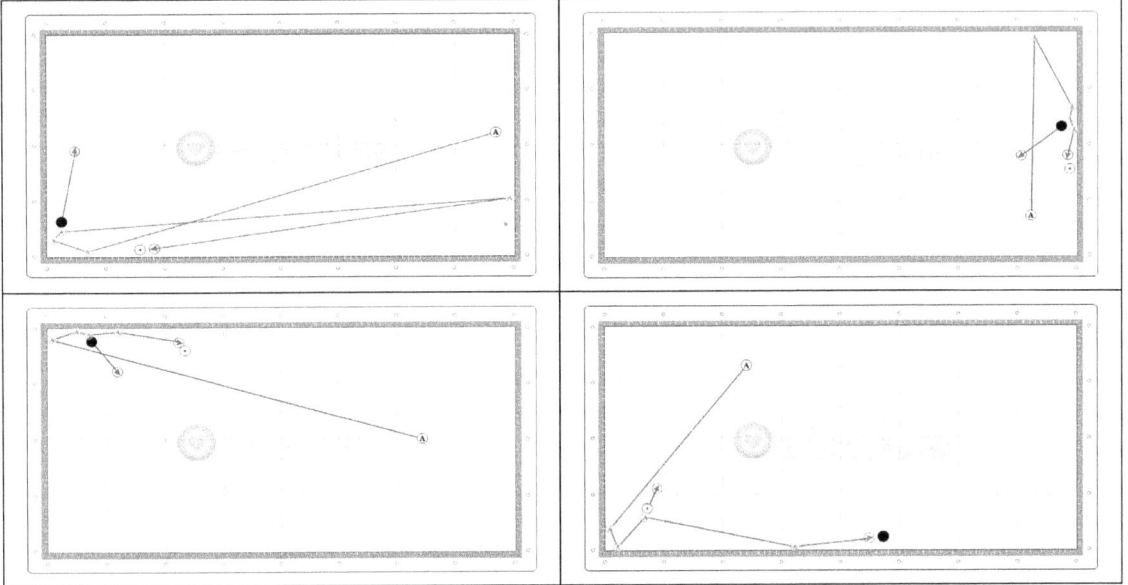

Analysis:

C:2a. _____

C:2b. _____

C:2c. _____

C:2d. _____

C:2a – Setup

Shot Pattern

C:2b – Setup

Shot Pattern

C:2c – Setup

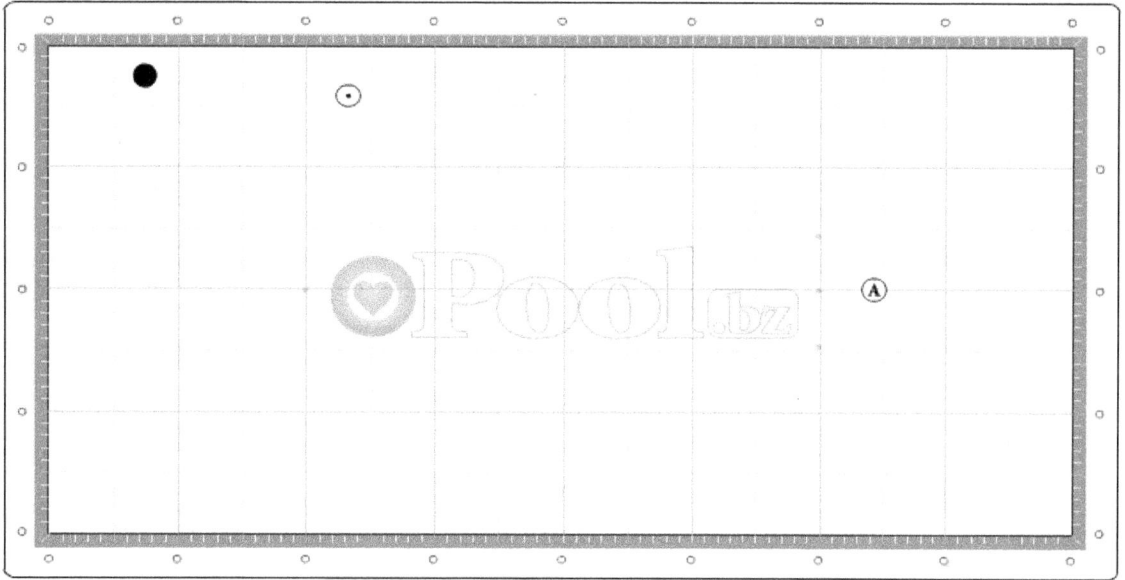

Shot Pattern

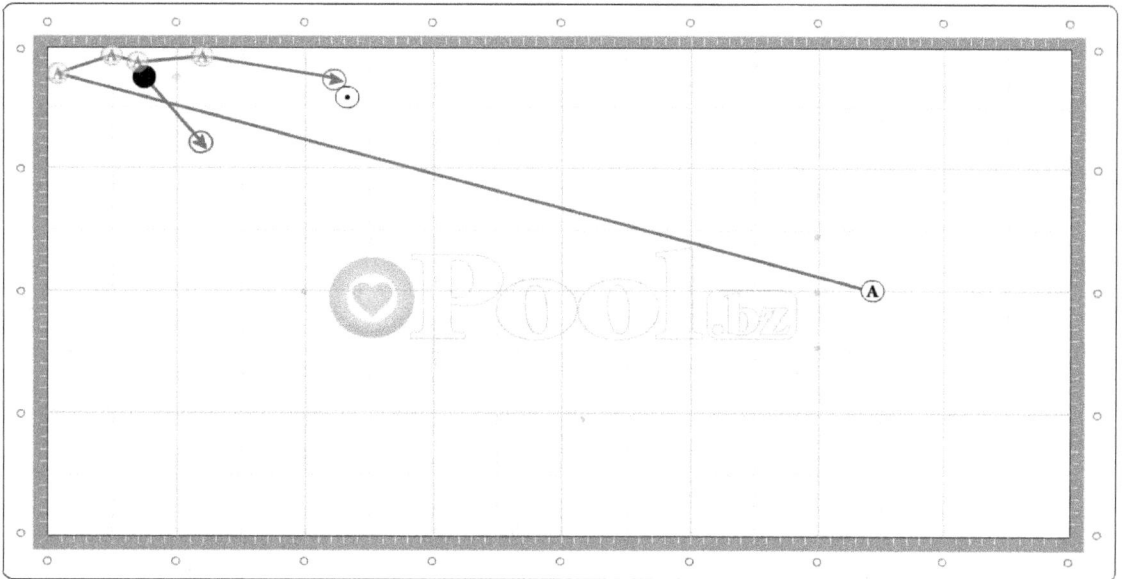

C:2d – Setup

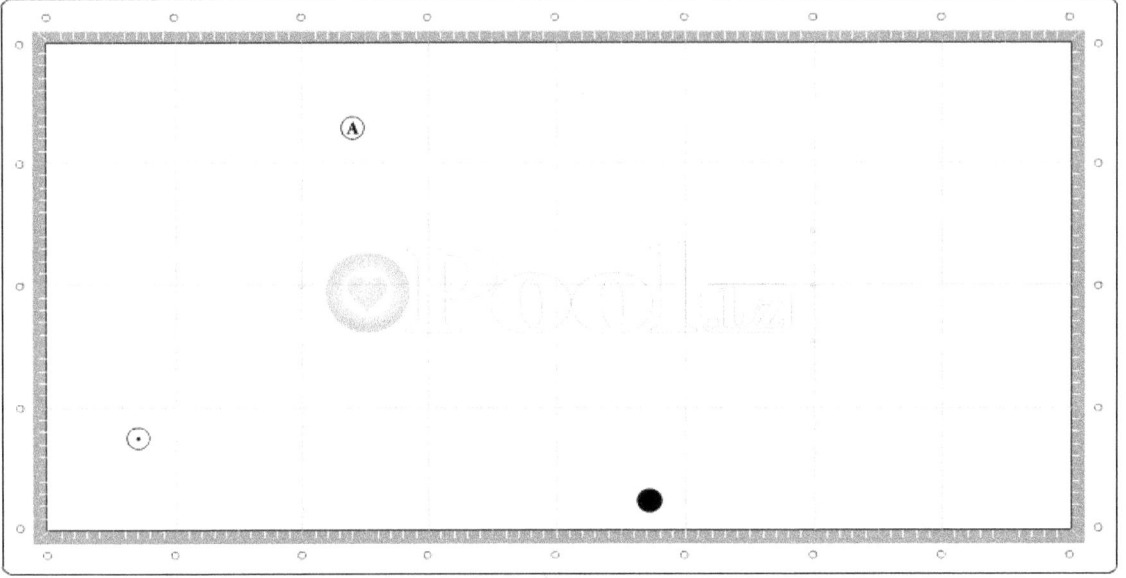

Shot Pattern

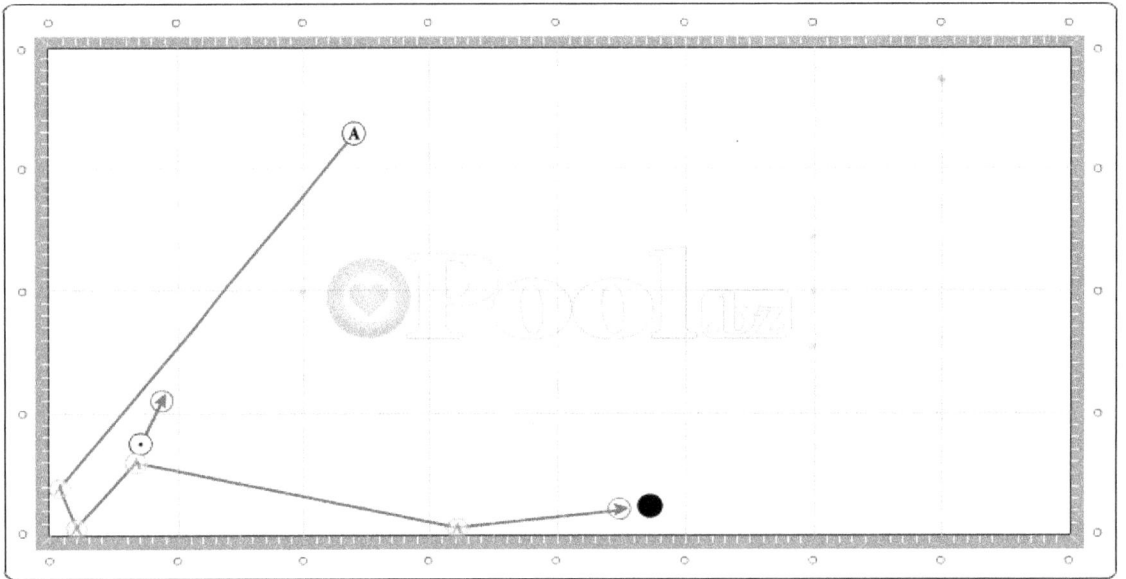

D: 3 cushions first, Series 1

Three-cushions first are more common. There shots have been divided into two sections to provide you with an extensive variety. For these shots, the CB follows a pattern that goes into three rails first. Then the CB contacts the first OB and the second OB for a successful shot.

D: Group 1

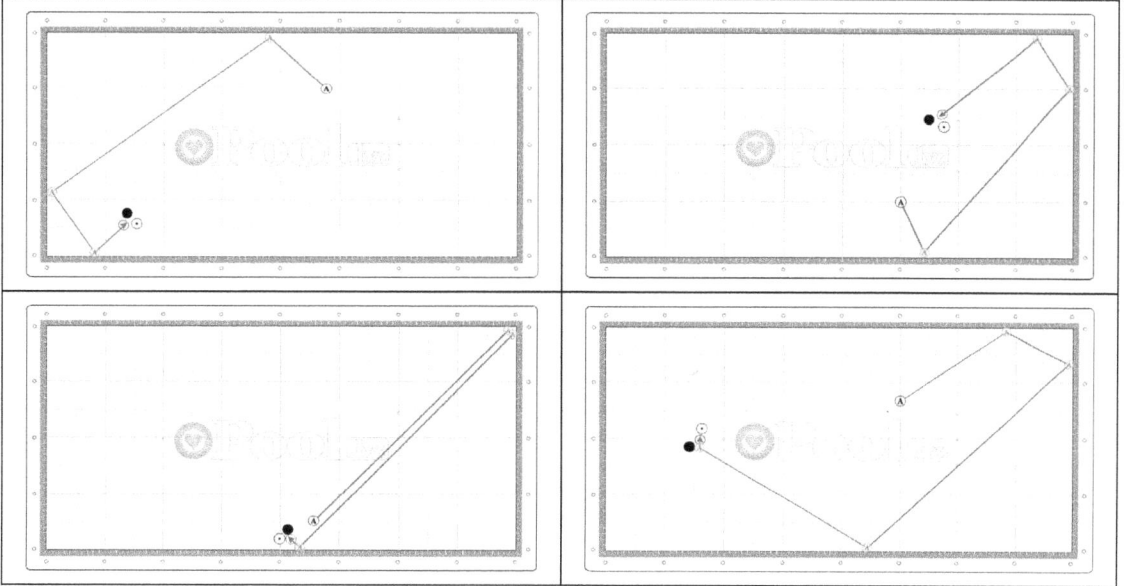

Analysis:

D:1a. _____

D:1b. _____

D:1c. _____

D:1d. _____

D:1a – Setup

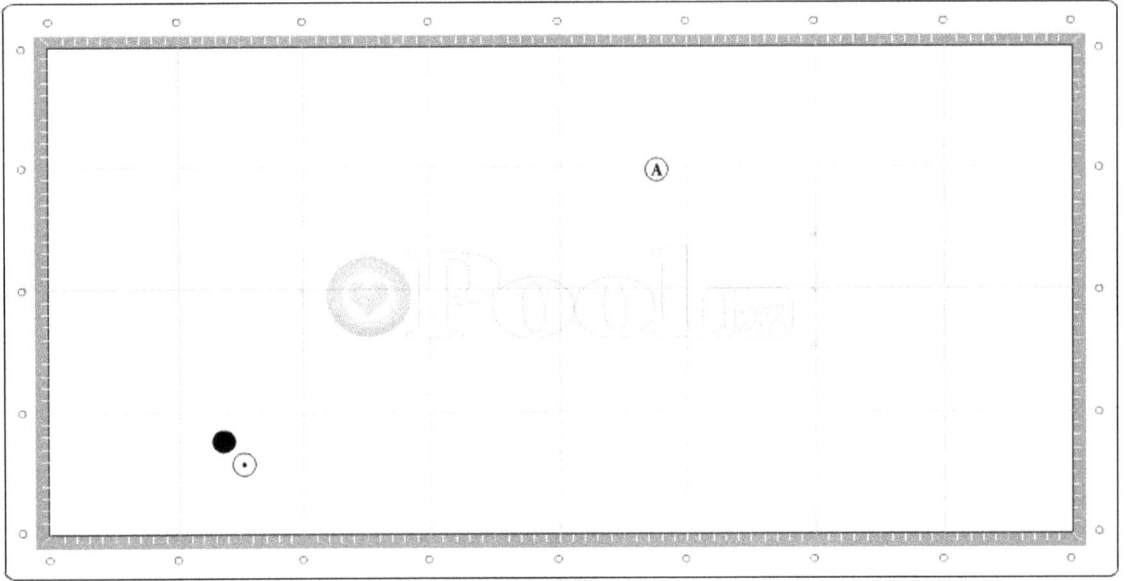

Shot Pattern

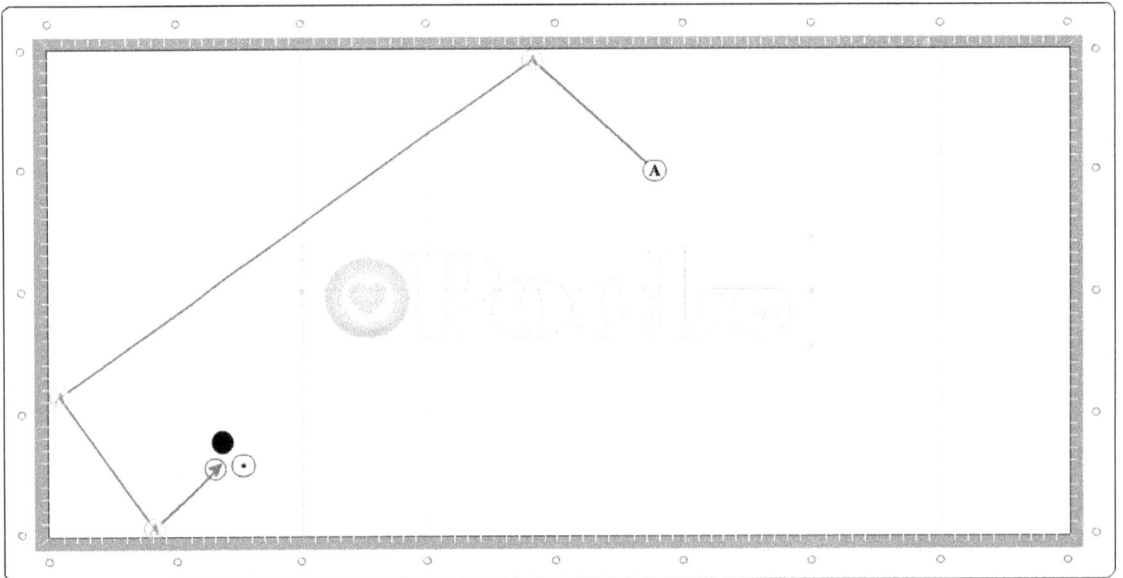

D:1b – Setup

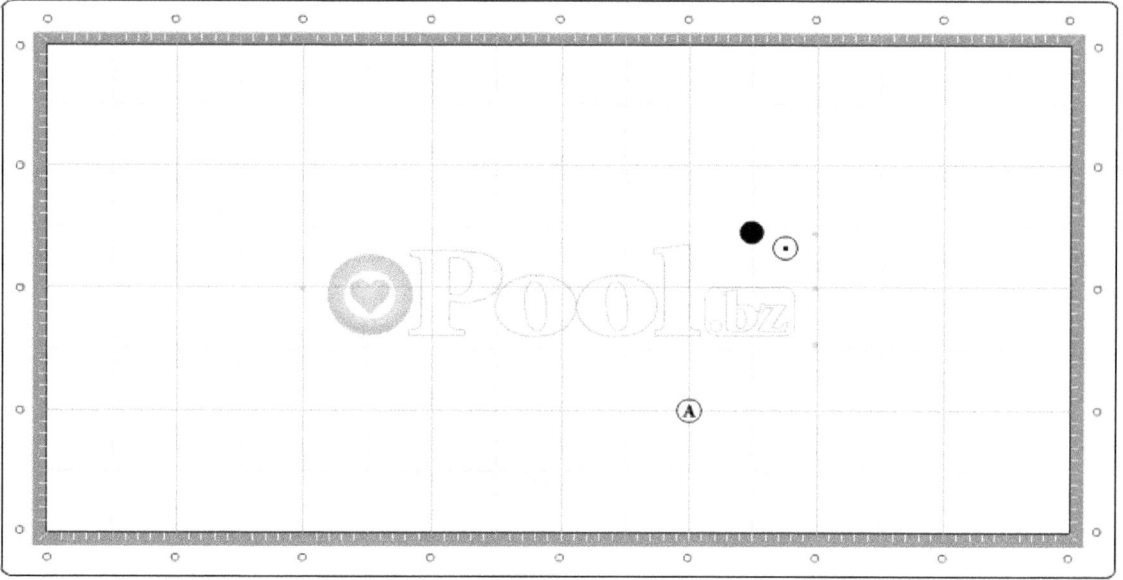

Shot Pattern

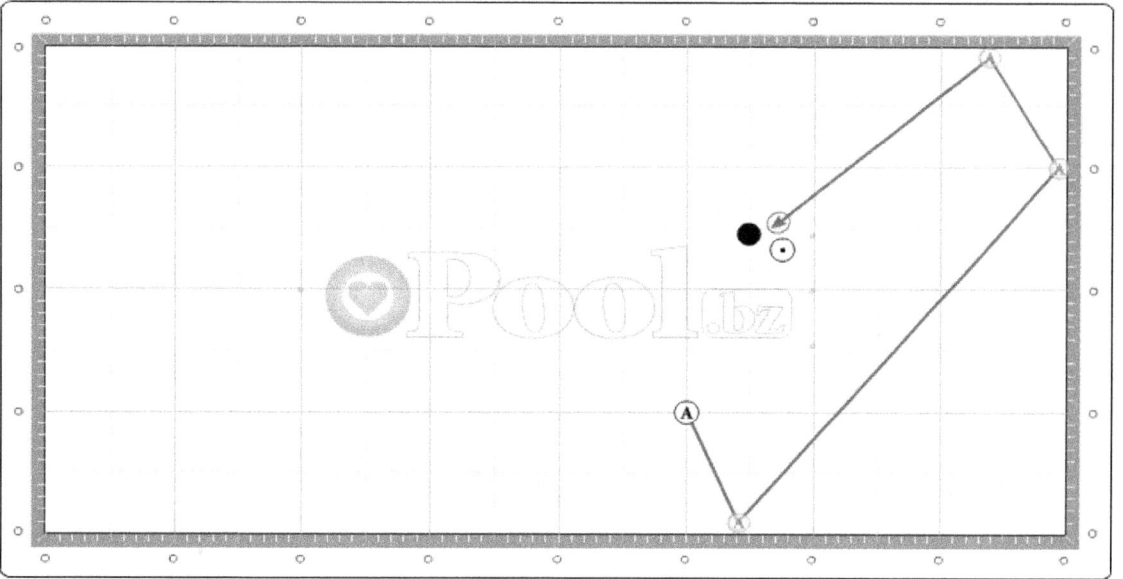

D:1c – Setup

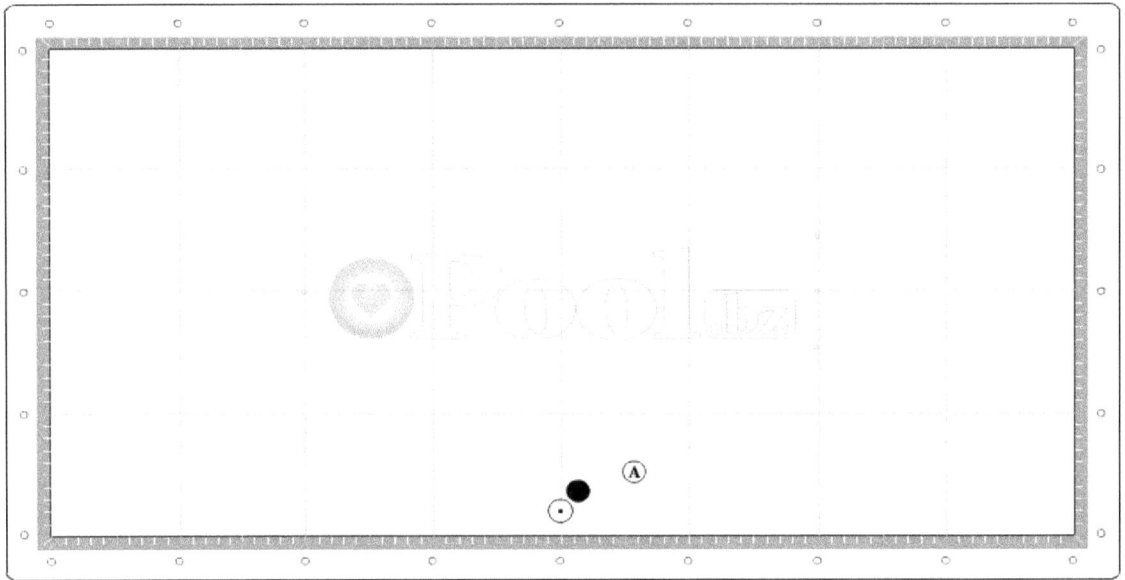

Shot Pattern

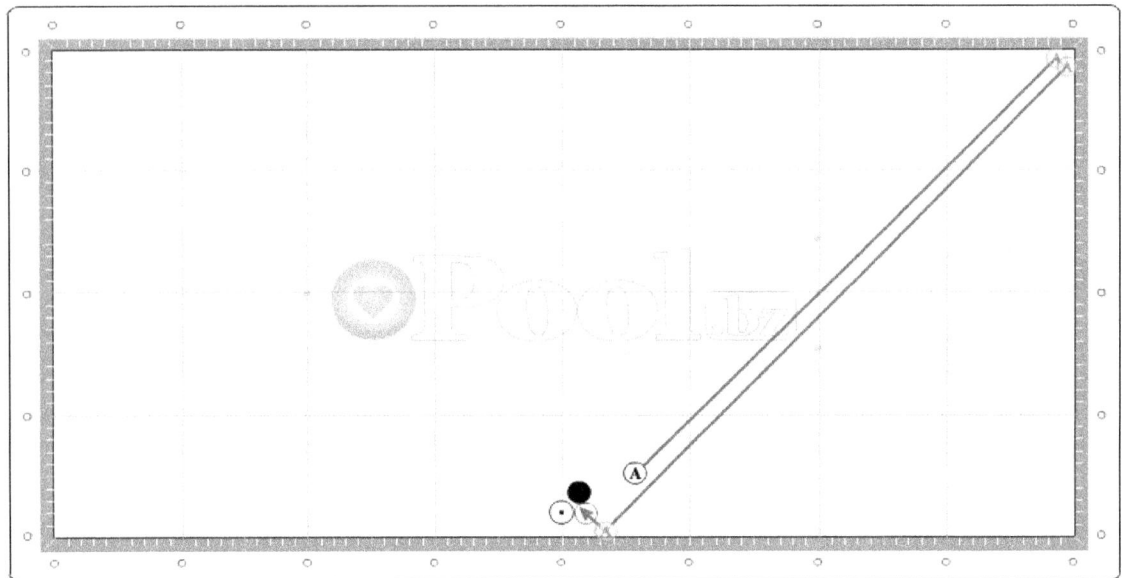

D:1d – Setup

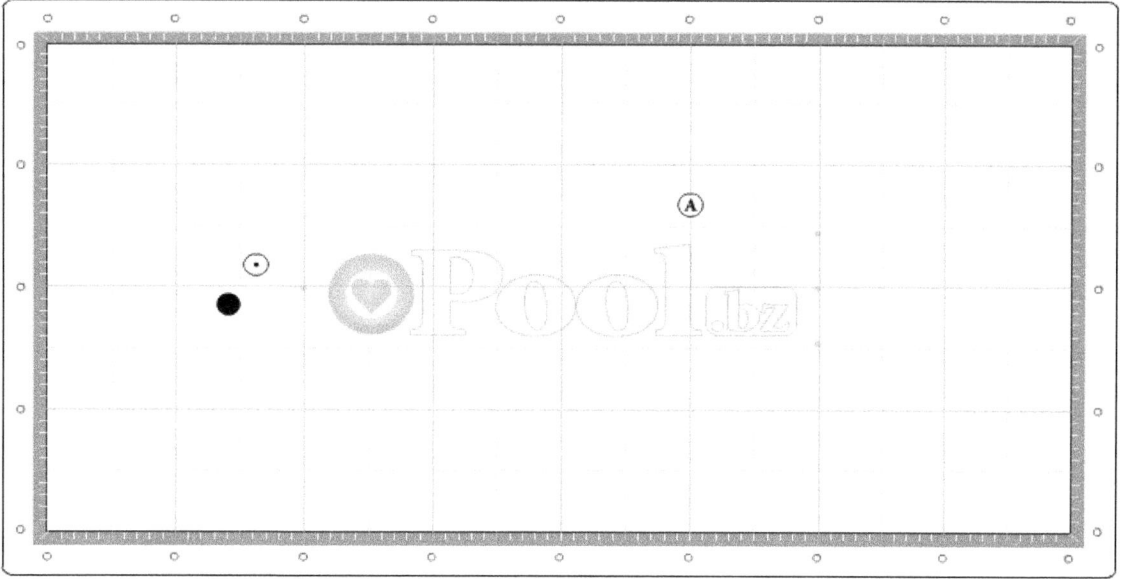

Shot Pattern

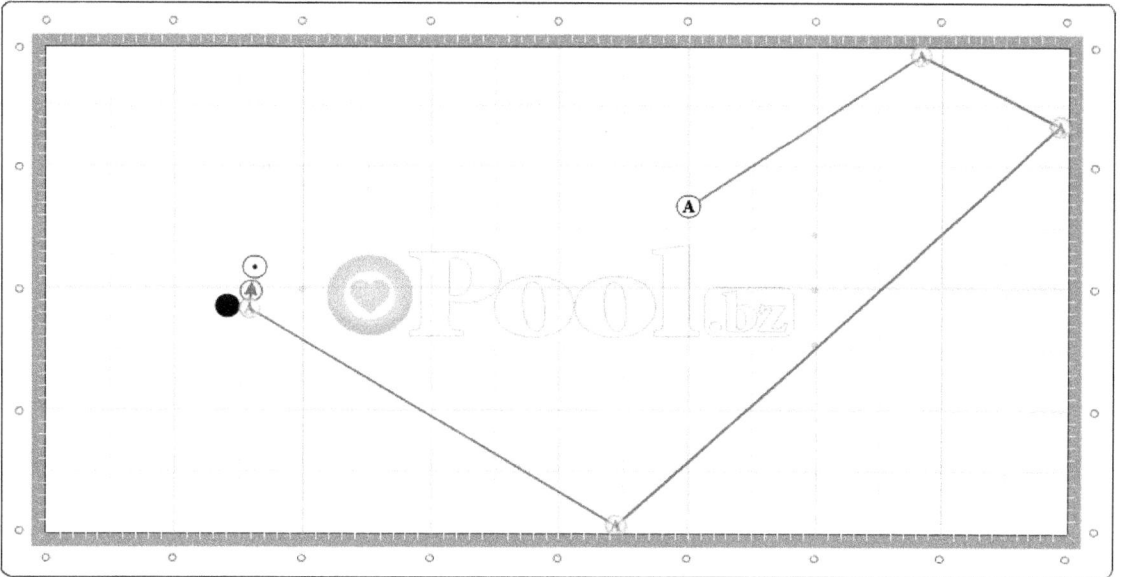

D: Group 2

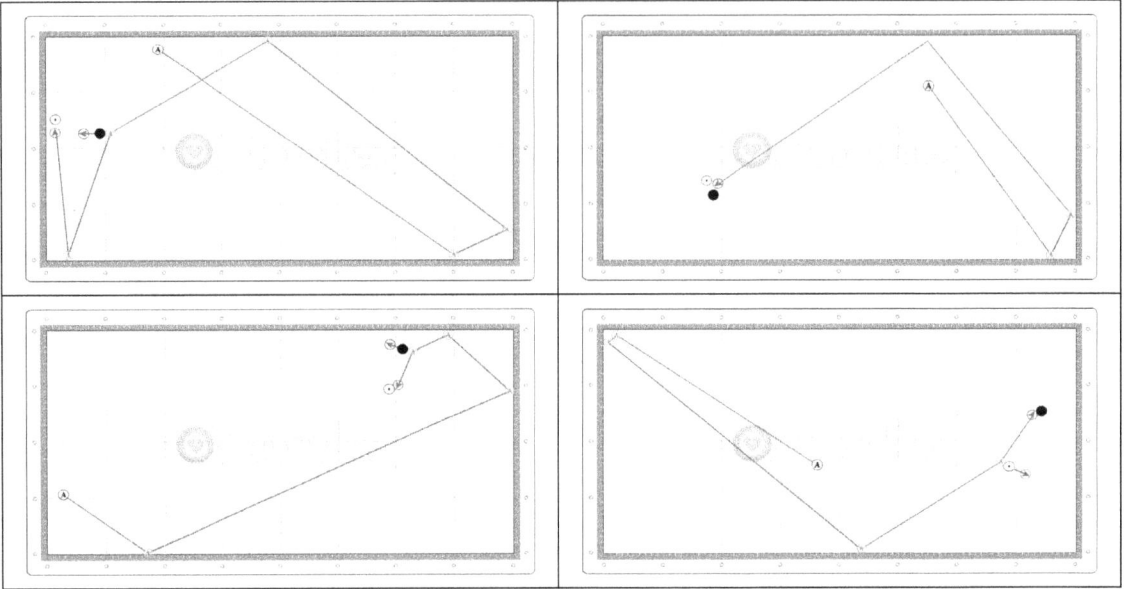

Analysis:

D:2a. _____

D:2b. _____

D:2c. _____

D:2d. _____

D:2a – Setup

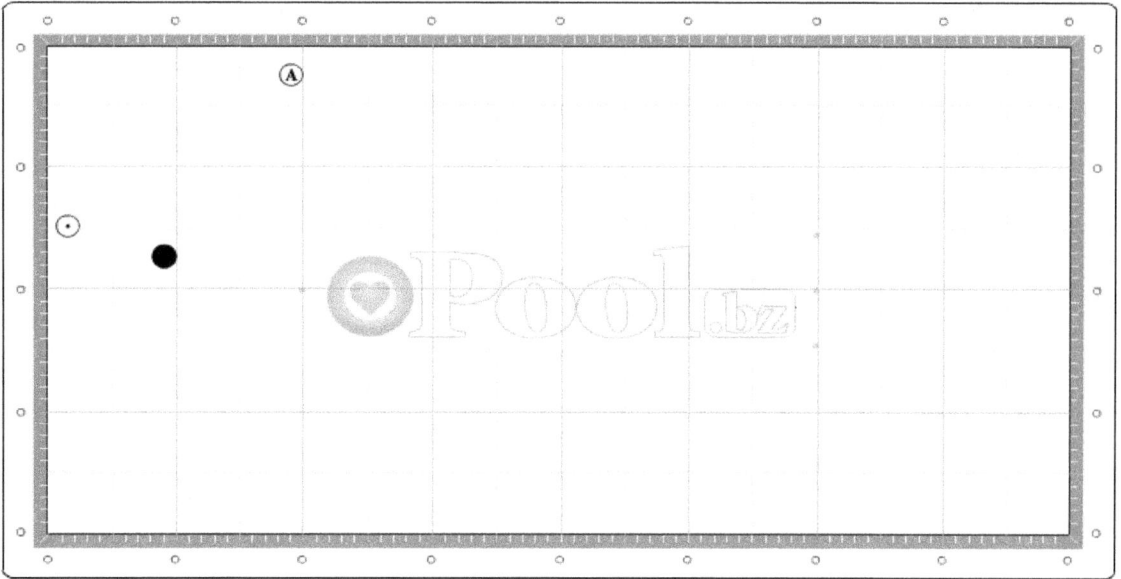

Shot Pattern

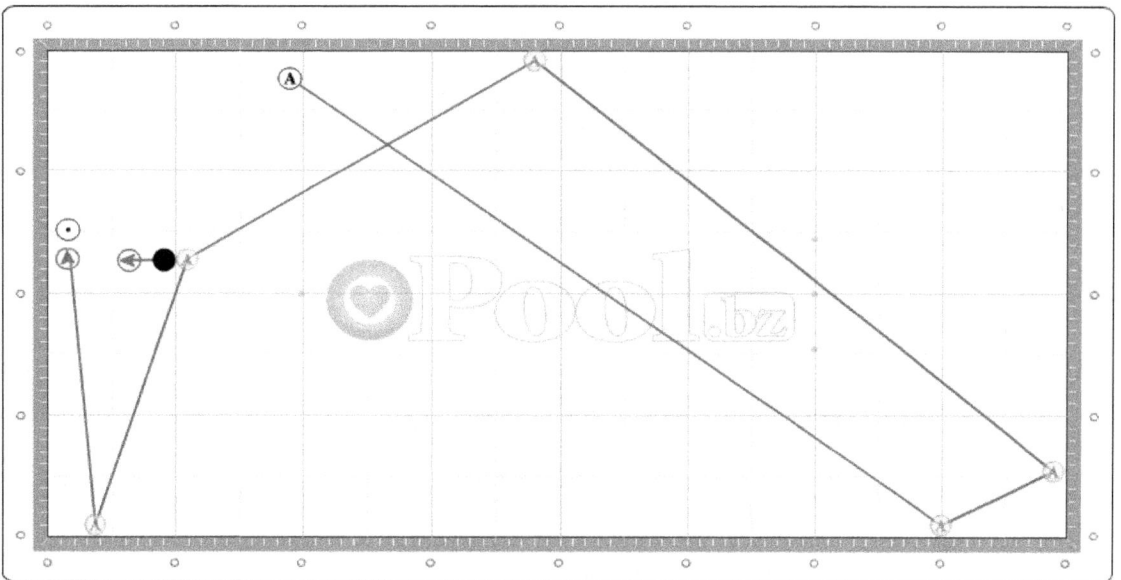

D:2b – Setup

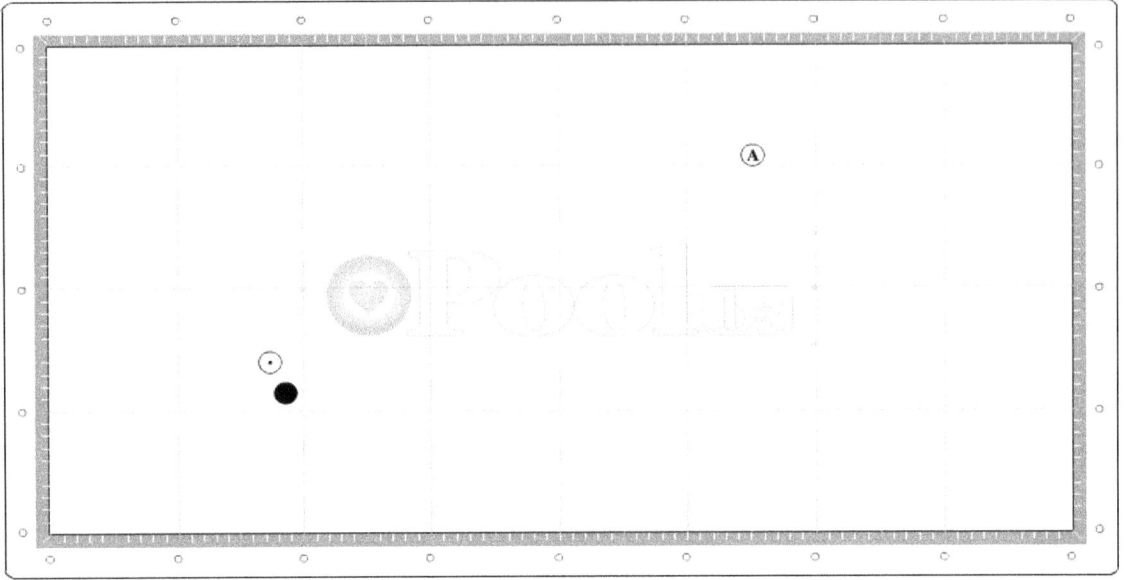

Shot Pattern

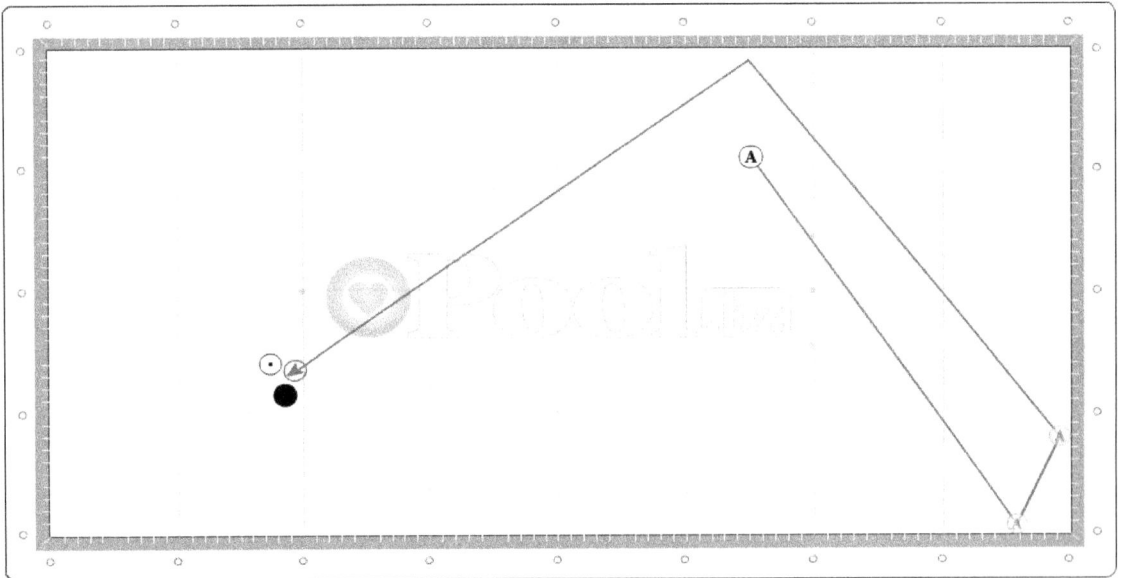

D:2c – Setup

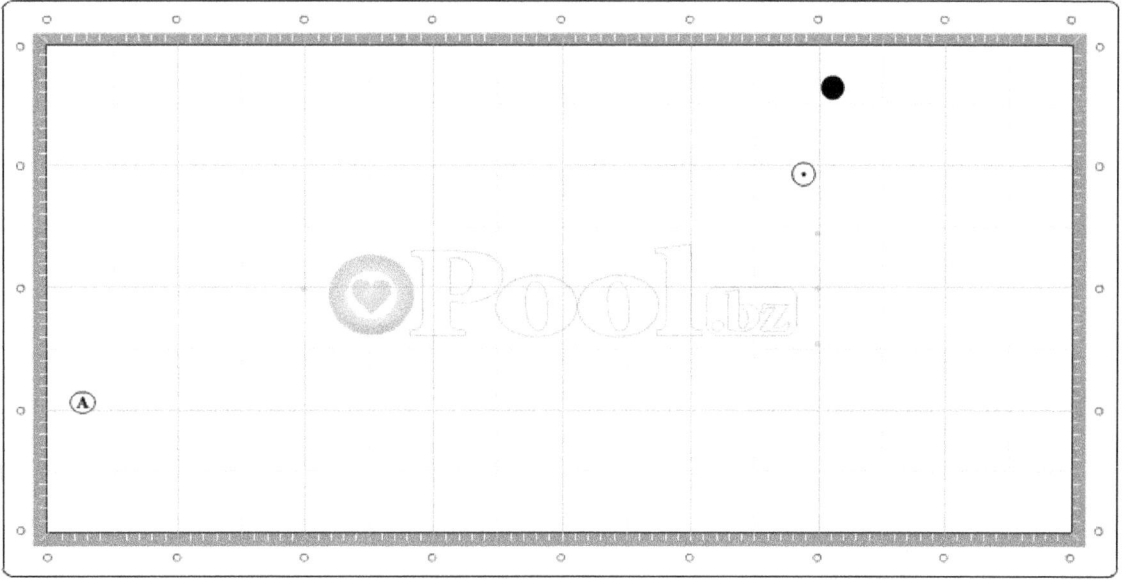

Shot Pattern

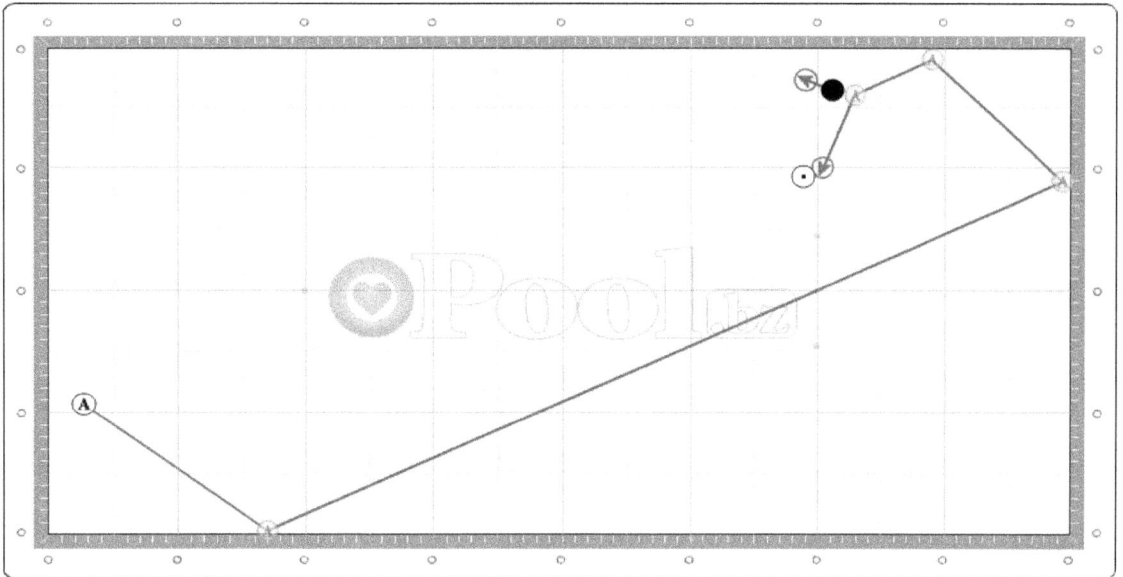

D:2d – Setup

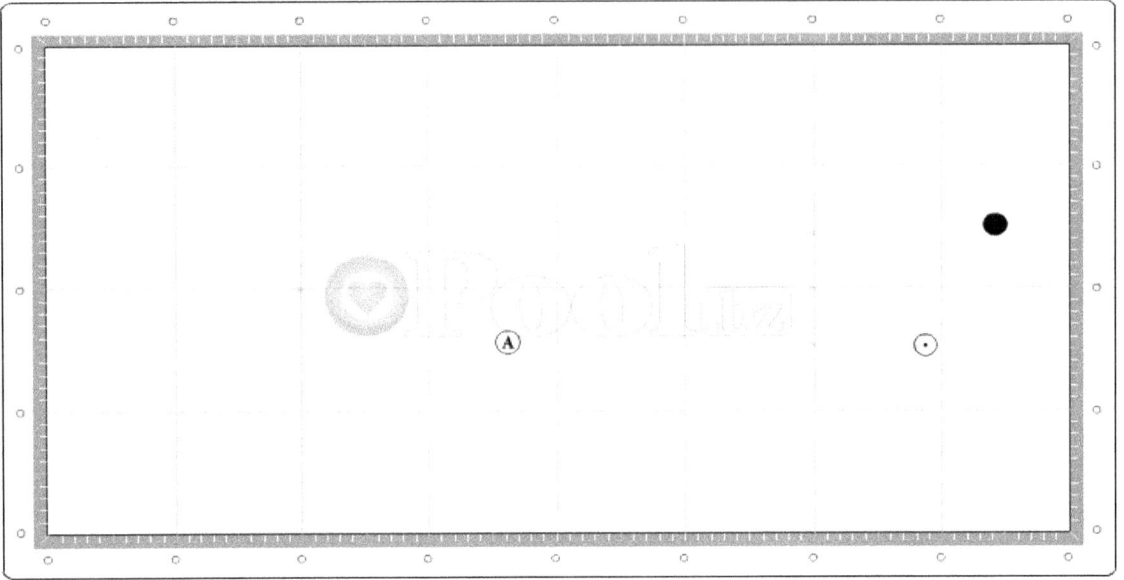

Shot Pattern

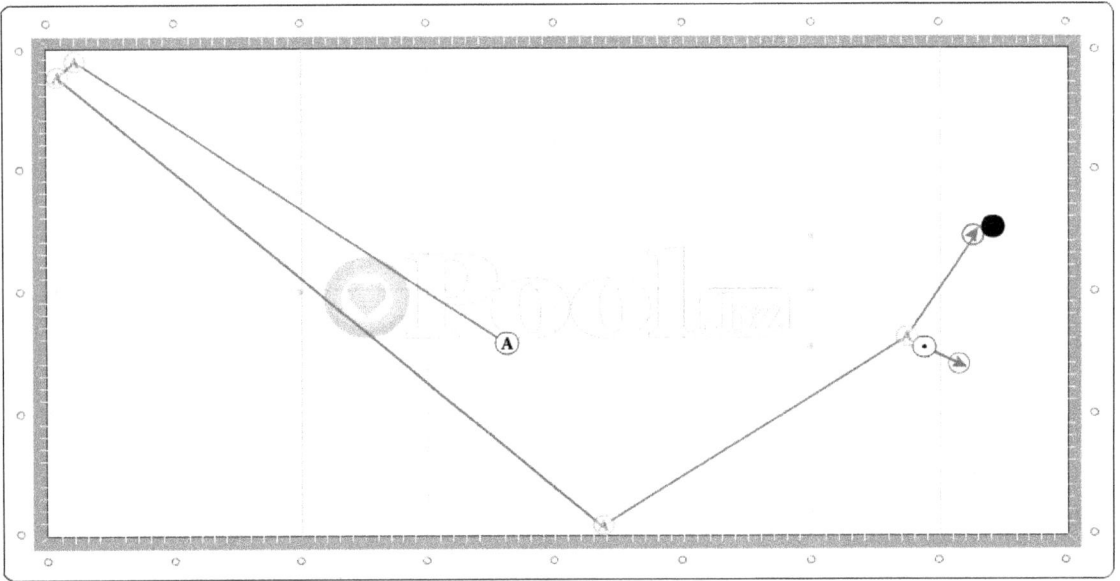

D: Group 3

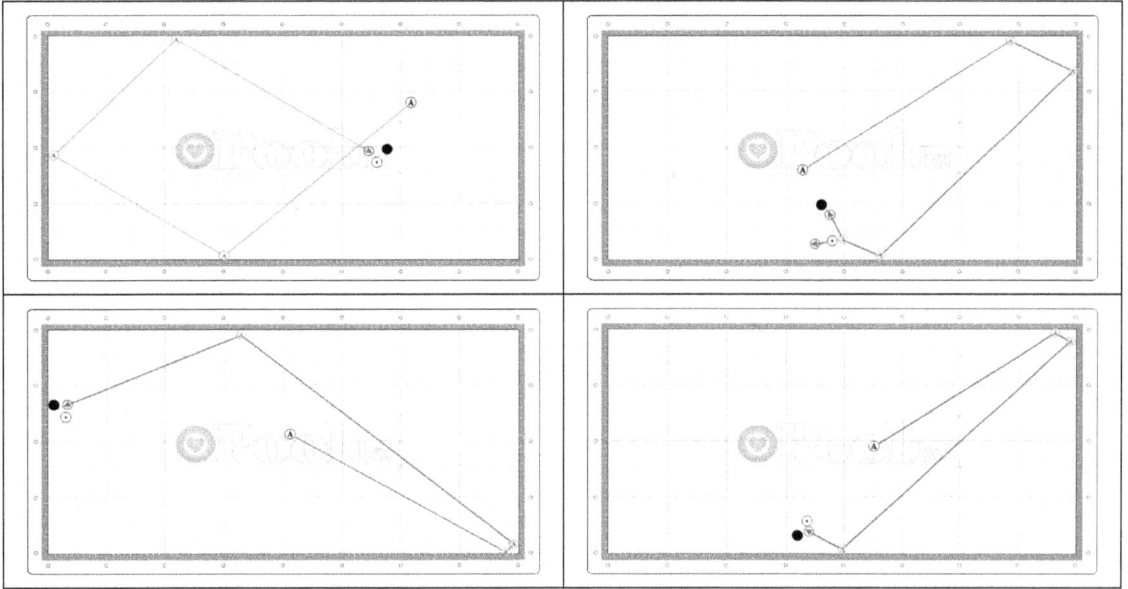

Analysis:

D:3a. _____

D:3b. _____

D:3c. _____

D:3d. _____

D:3a – Setup

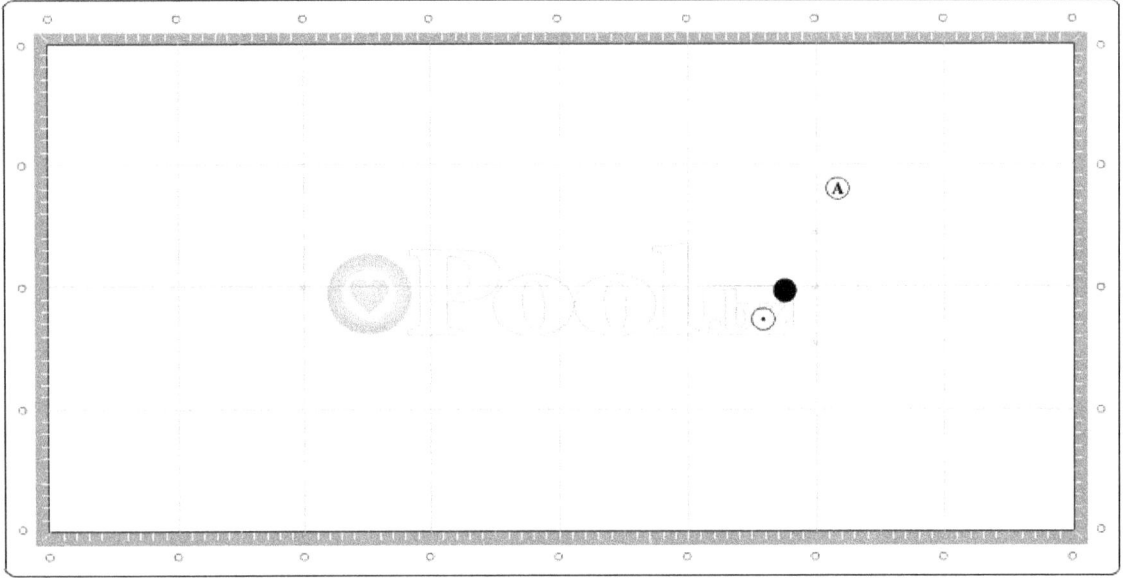

Shot Pattern

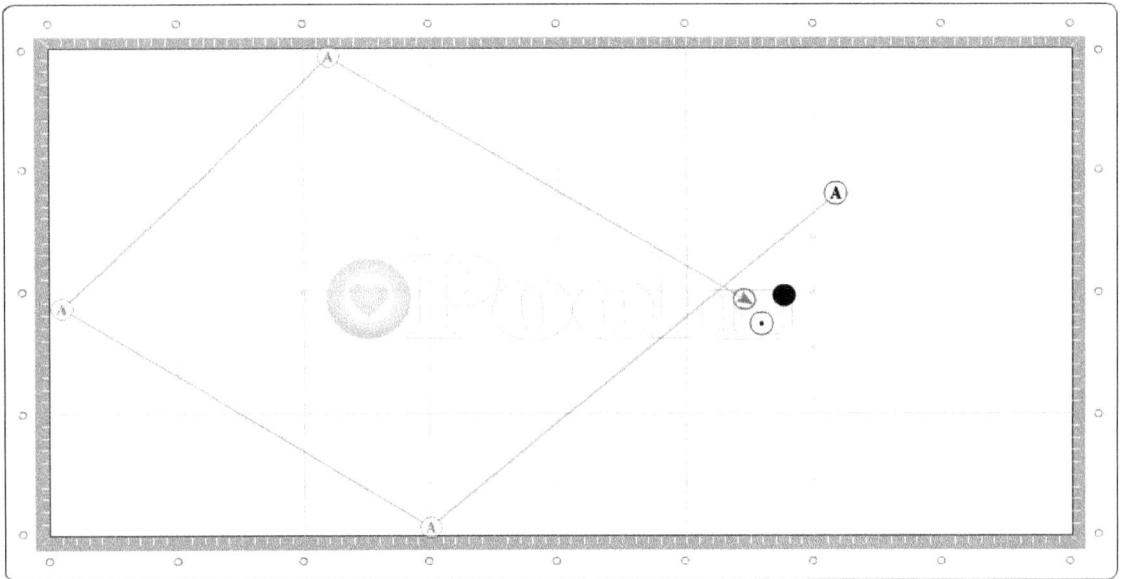

D:3b – Setup

Shot Pattern

D:3c – Setup

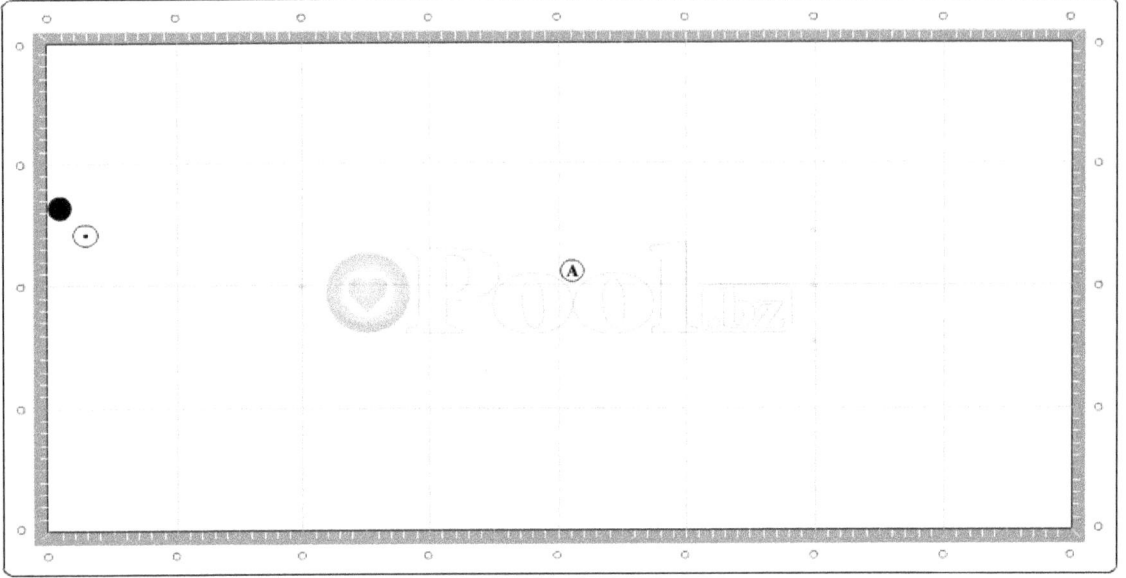

Shot Pattern

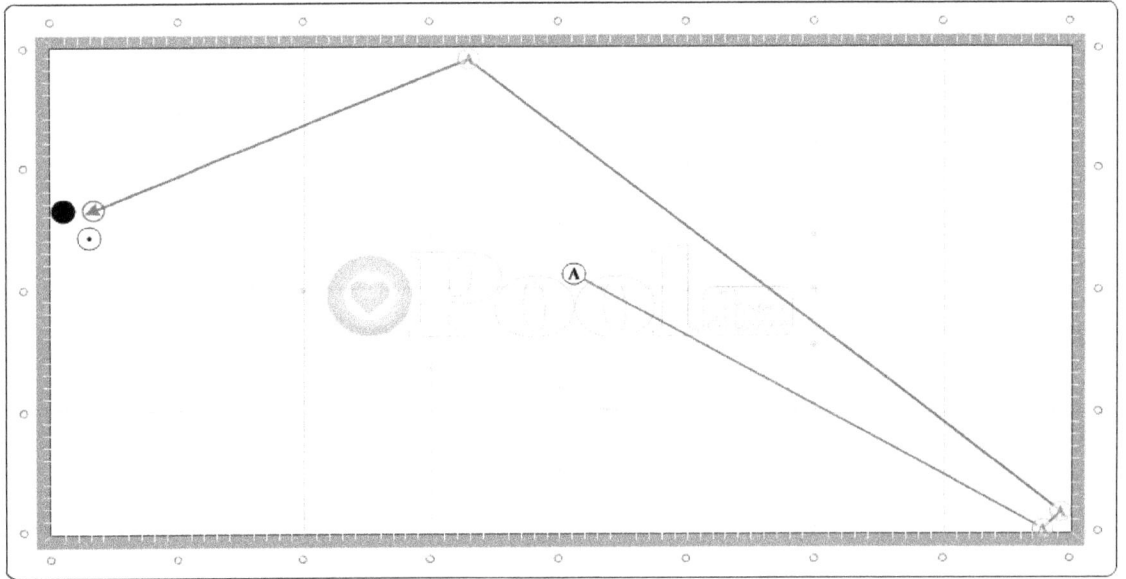

D:3d – Setup

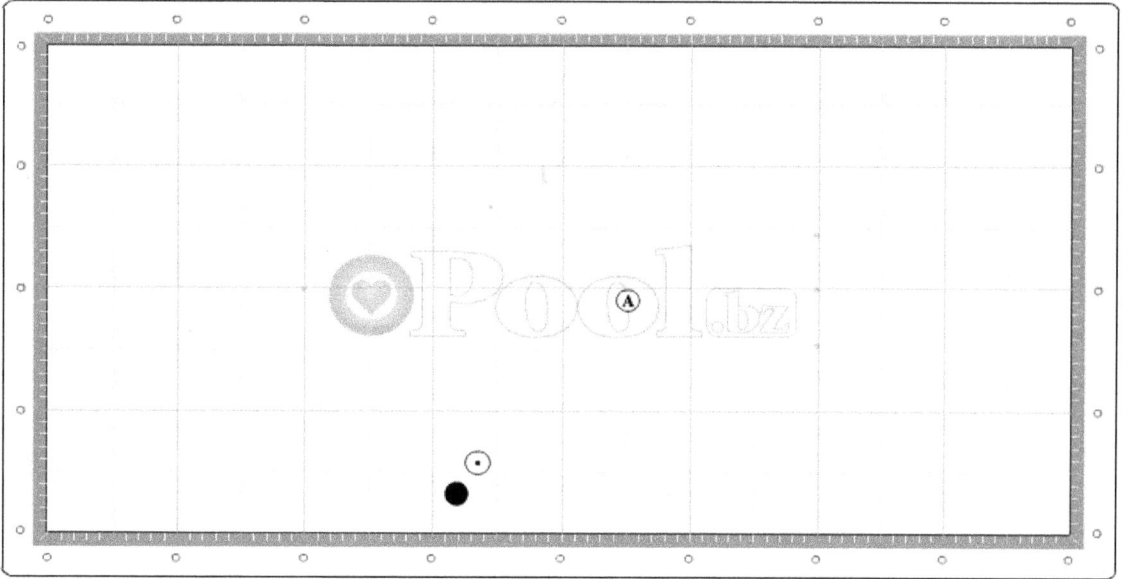

Shot Pattern

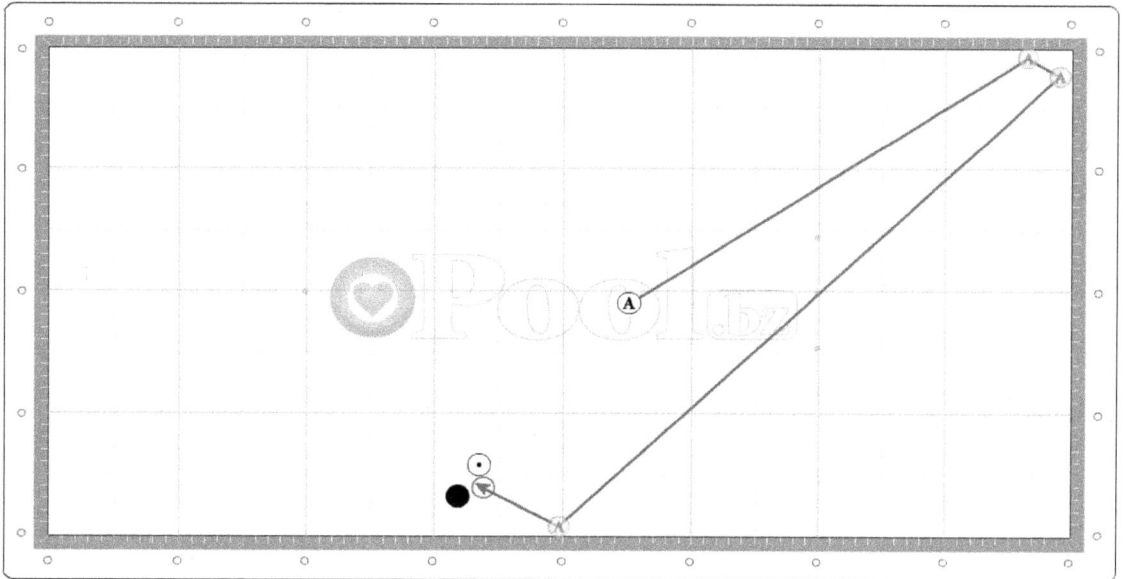

D: Group 4

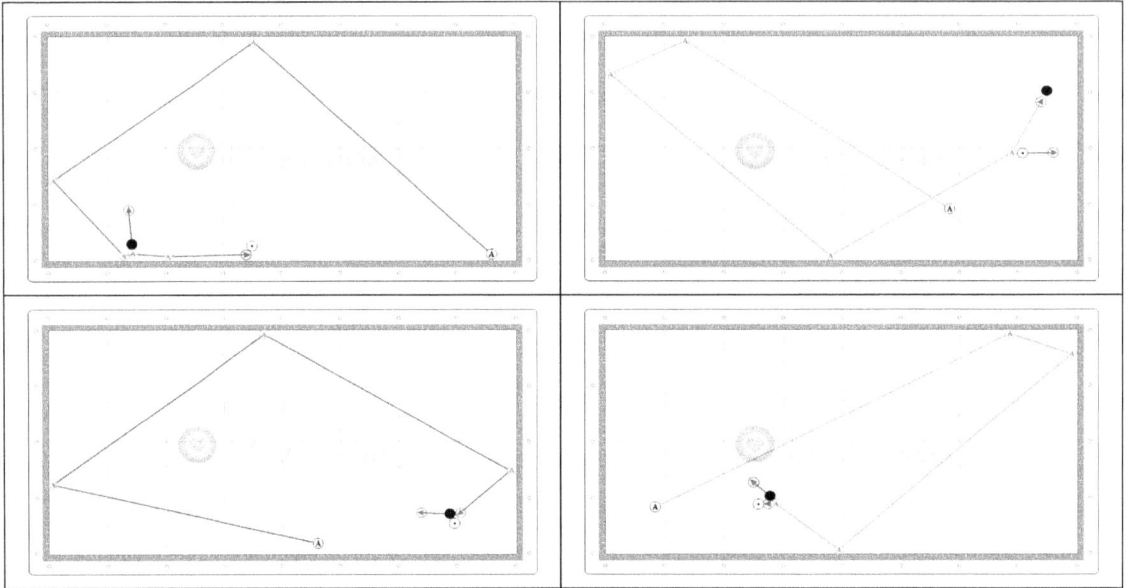

Analysis:

D:4a. _____

D:4b. _____

D:4c. _____

D:4d. _____

D:4a – Setup

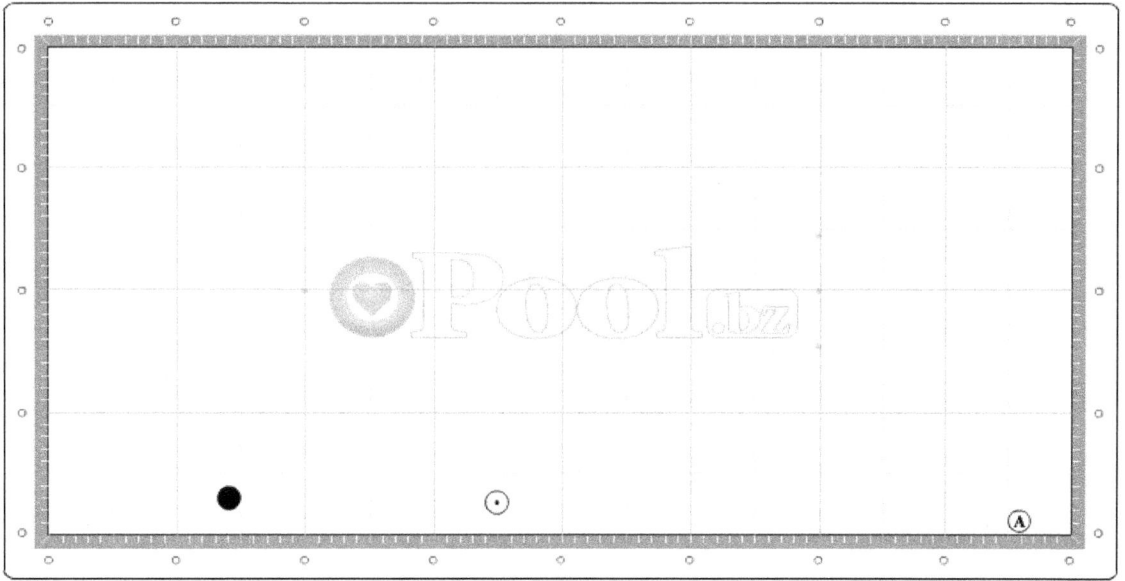

Shot Pattern

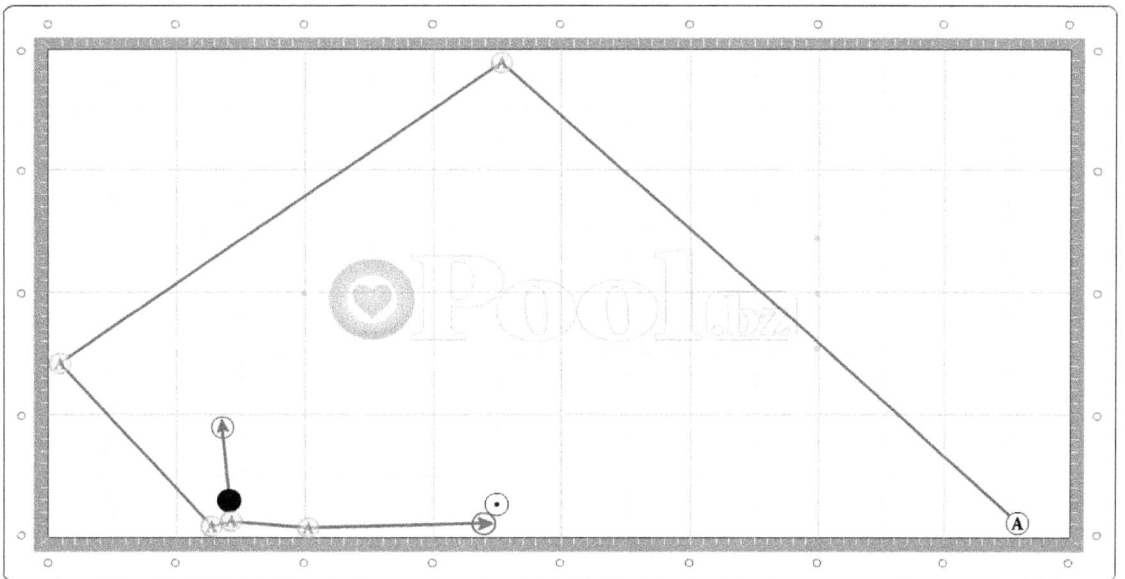

D:4b – Setup

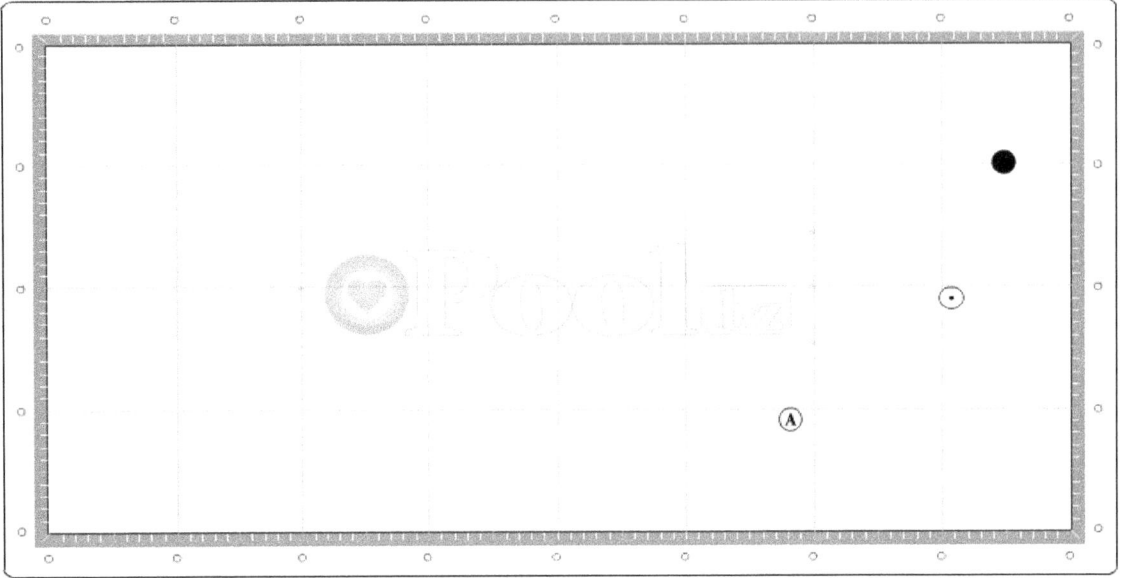

Shot Pattern

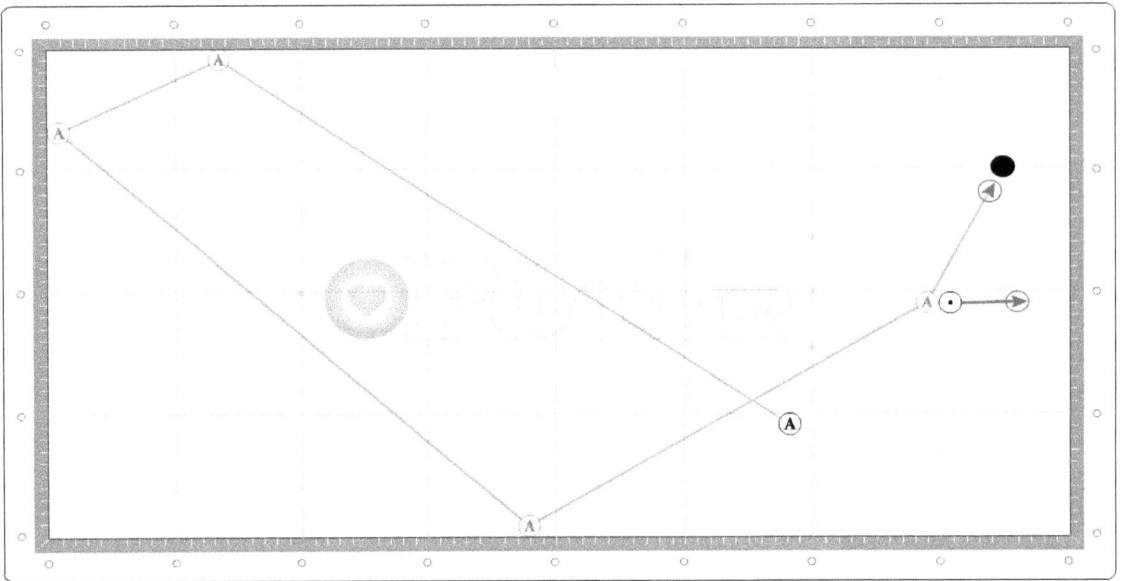

D:4c – Setup

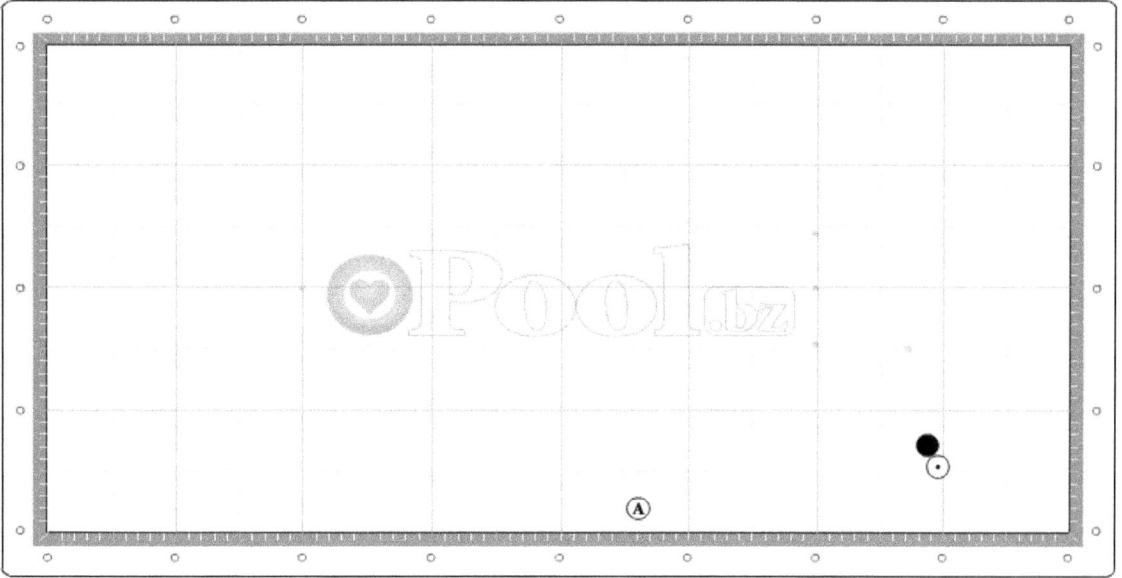

Shot Pattern

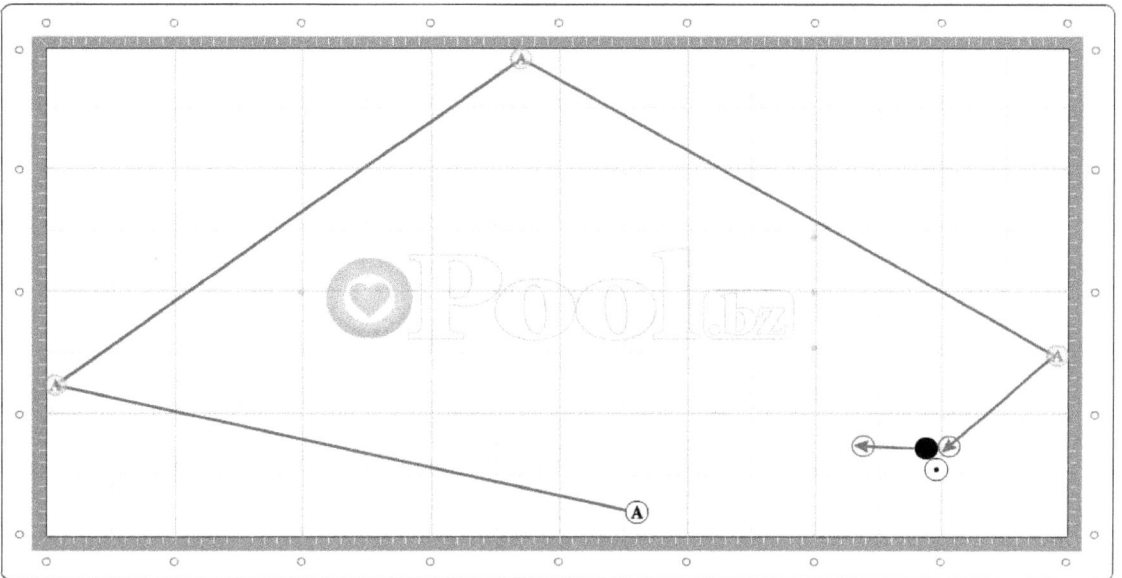

D:4d – Setup

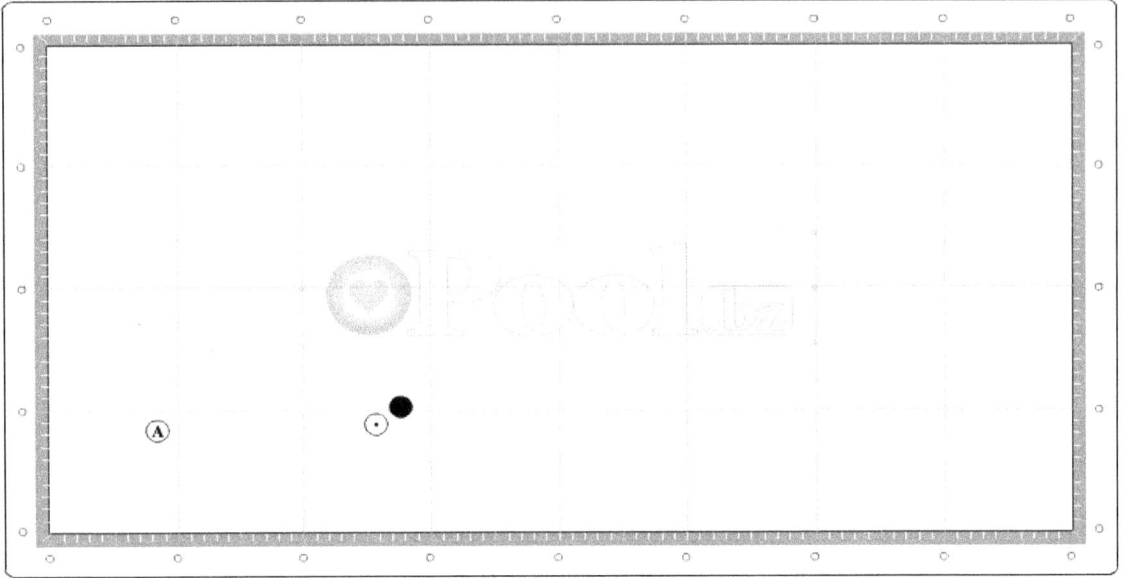

Shot Pattern

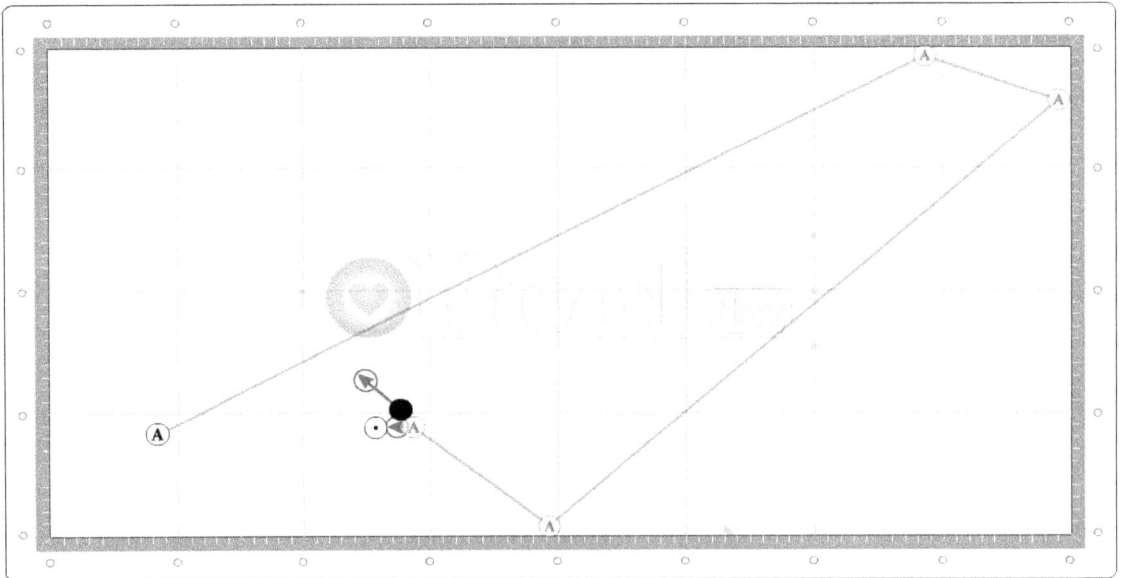

D: Group 5

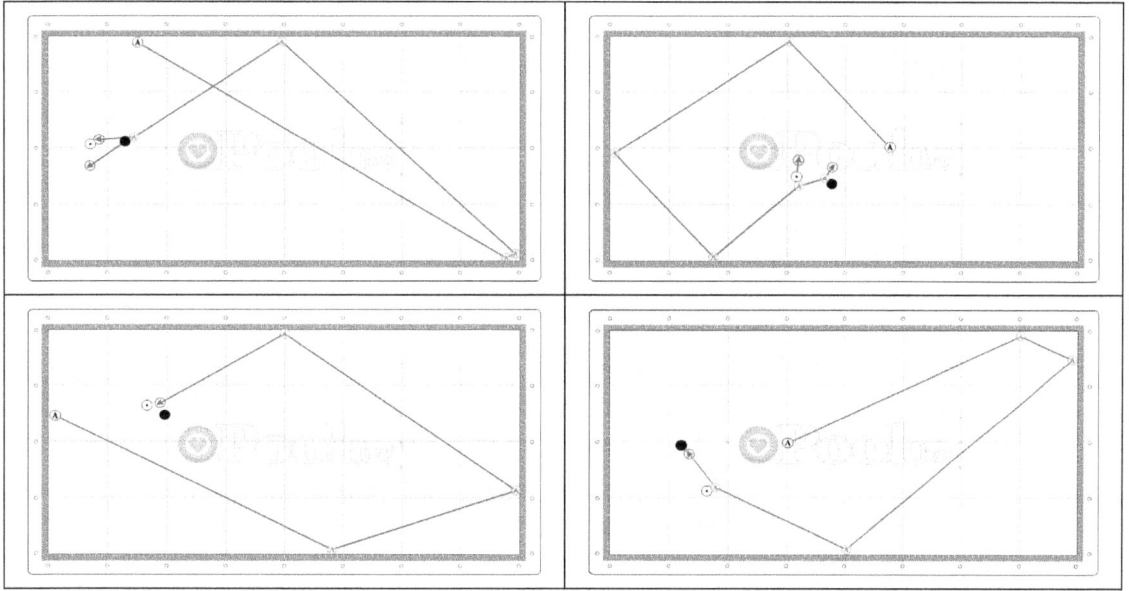

Analysis:

D:5a. _____

D:5b. _____

D:5c. _____

D:5d. _____

D:5a – Setup

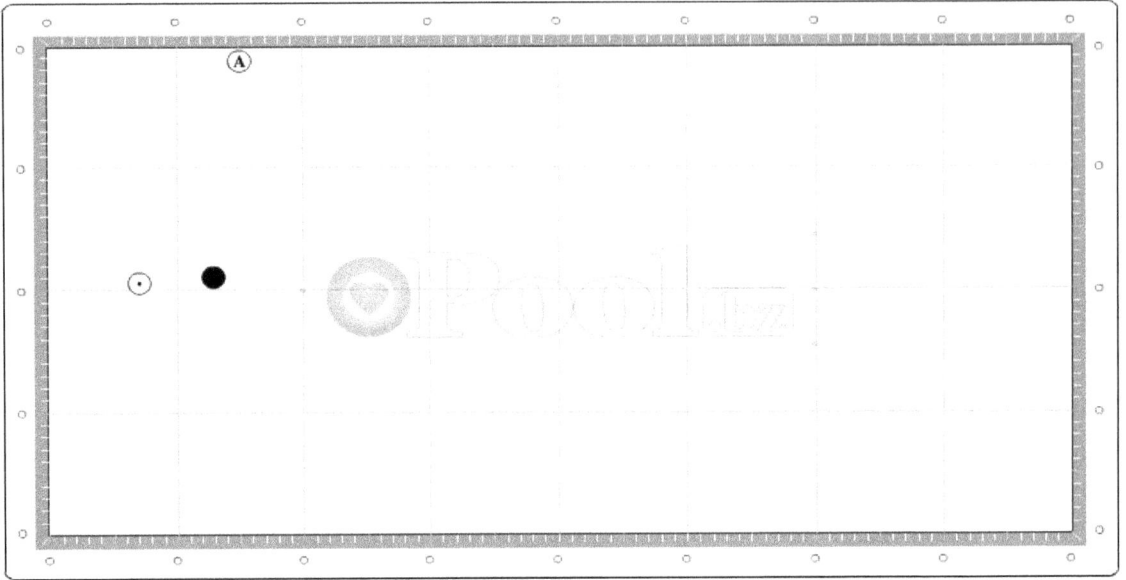

Shot Pattern

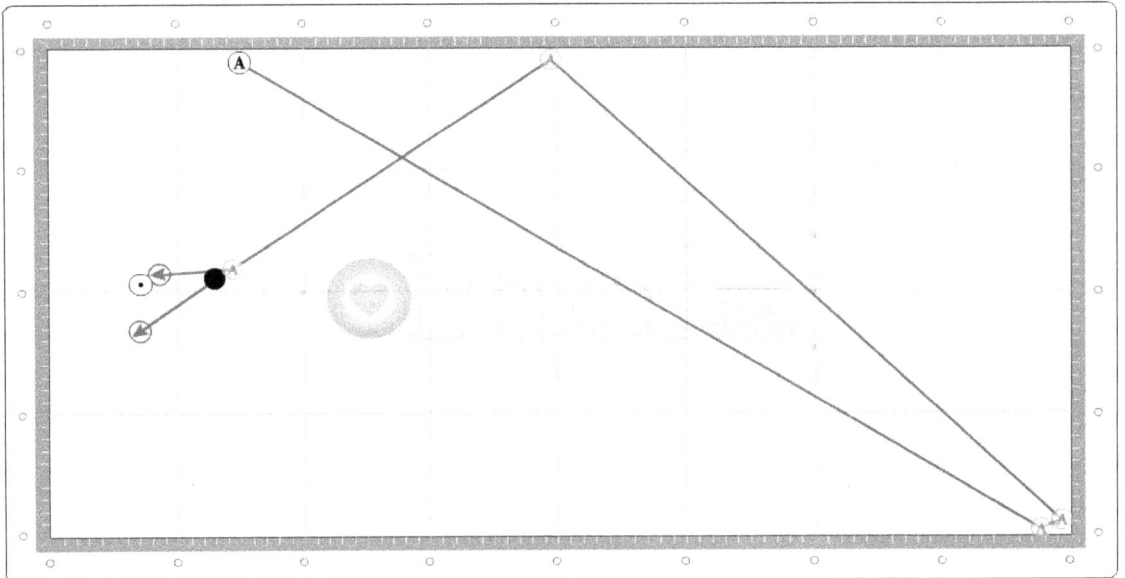

D:5b – Setup

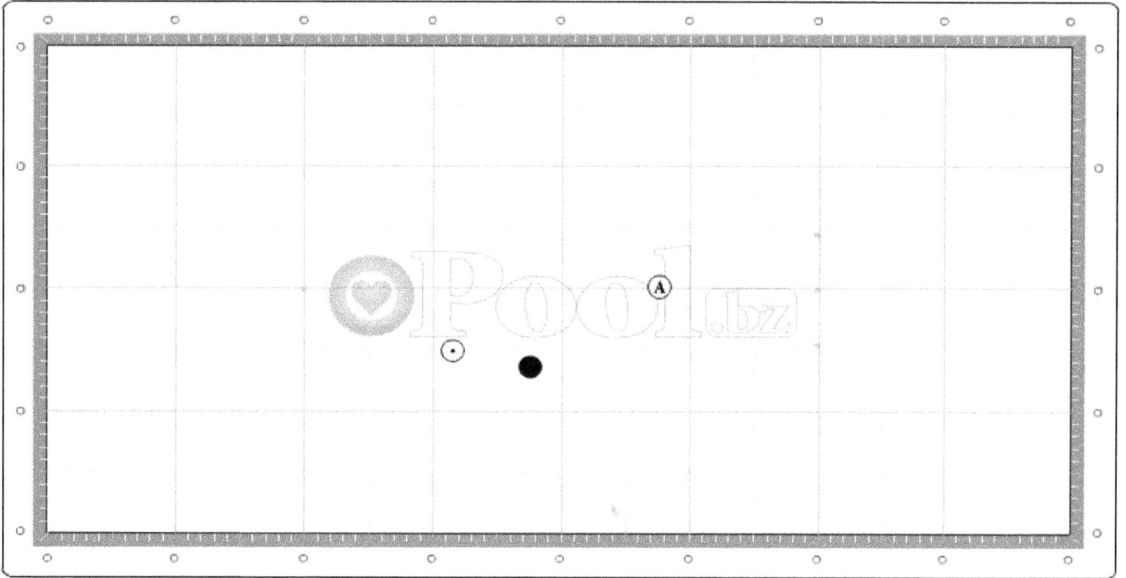

Shot Pattern

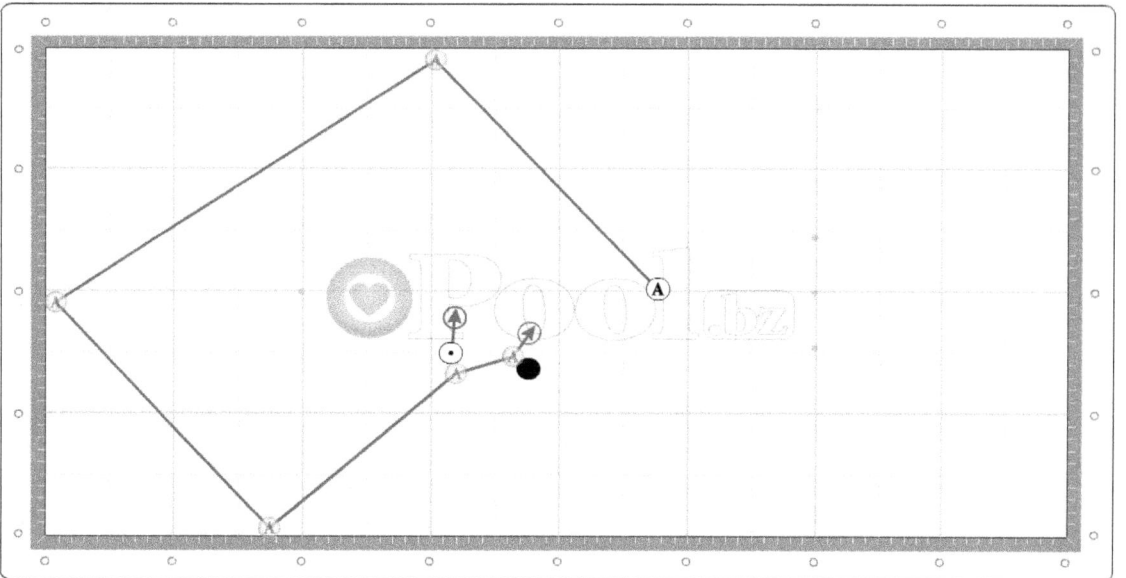

D:5c – Setup

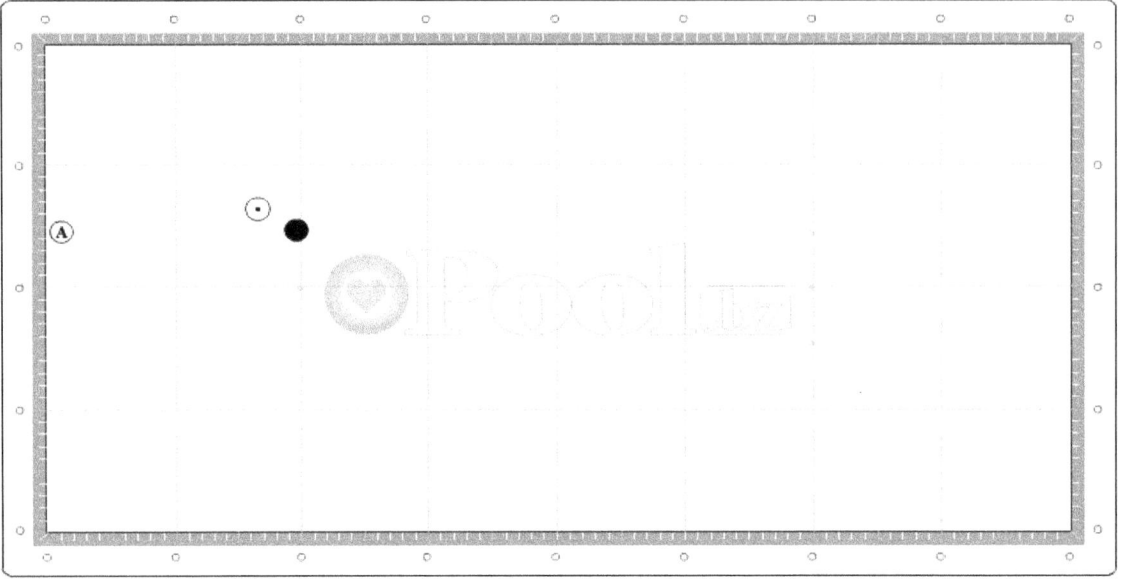

Shot Pattern

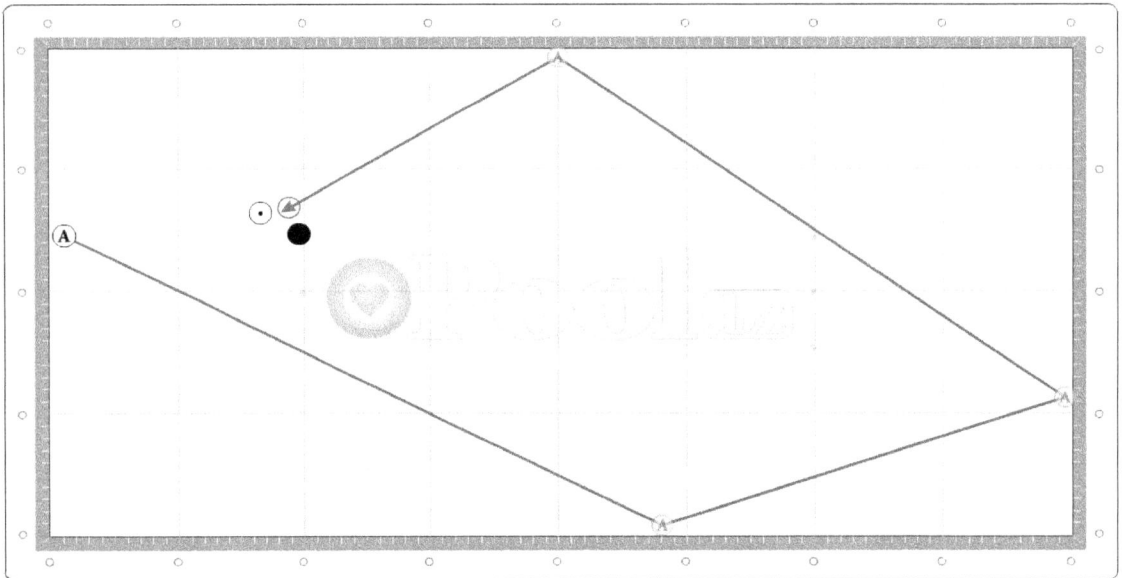

D:5d – Setup

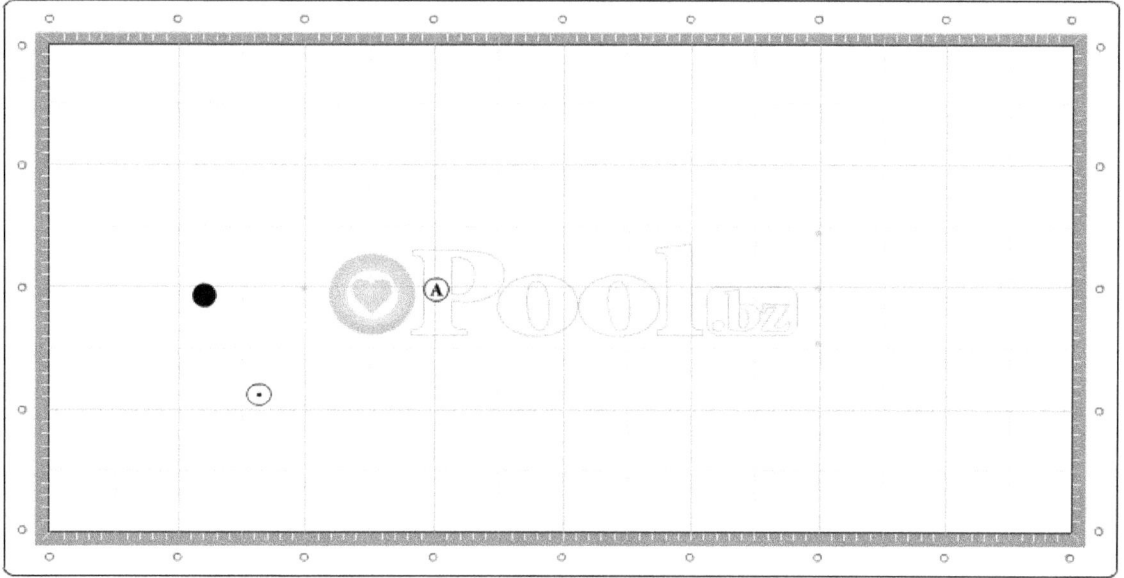

Shot Pattern

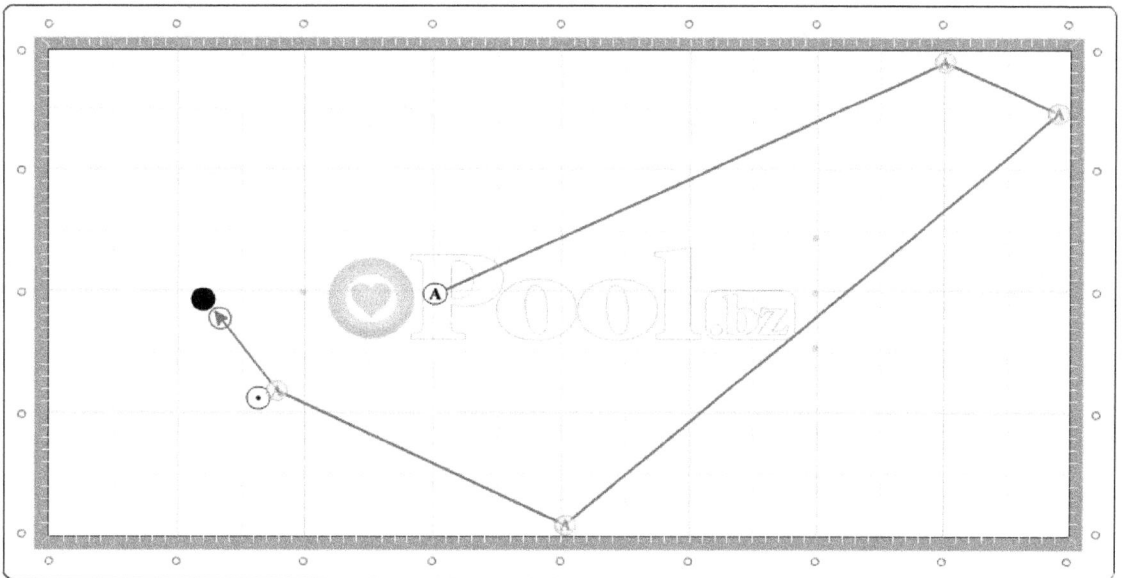

D: Group 6

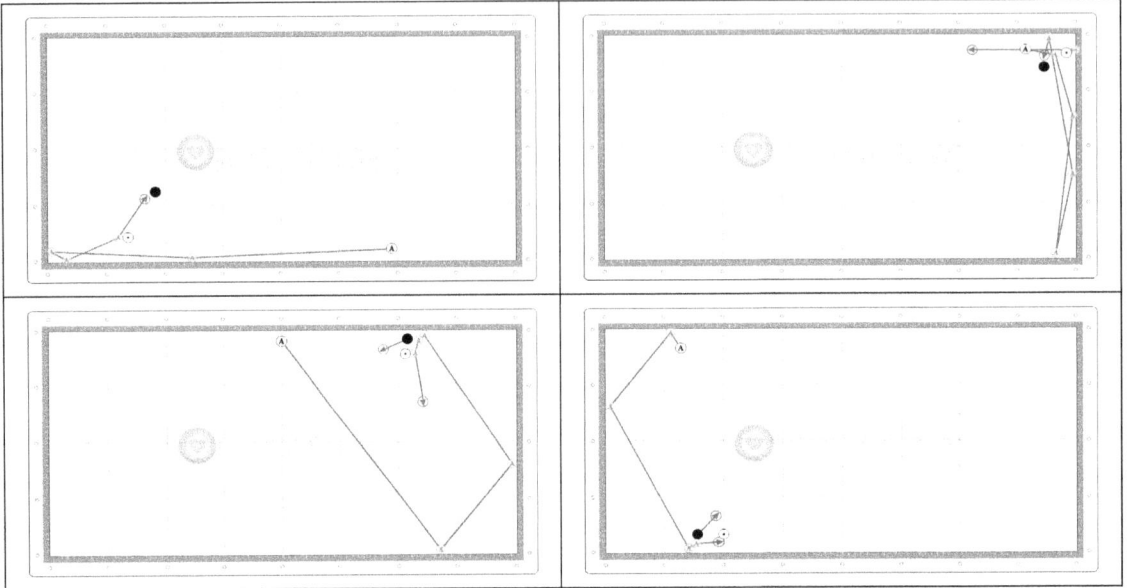

Analysis:

D:6a. _____

D:6b. _____

D:6c. _____

D:6d. _____

D:6a – Setup

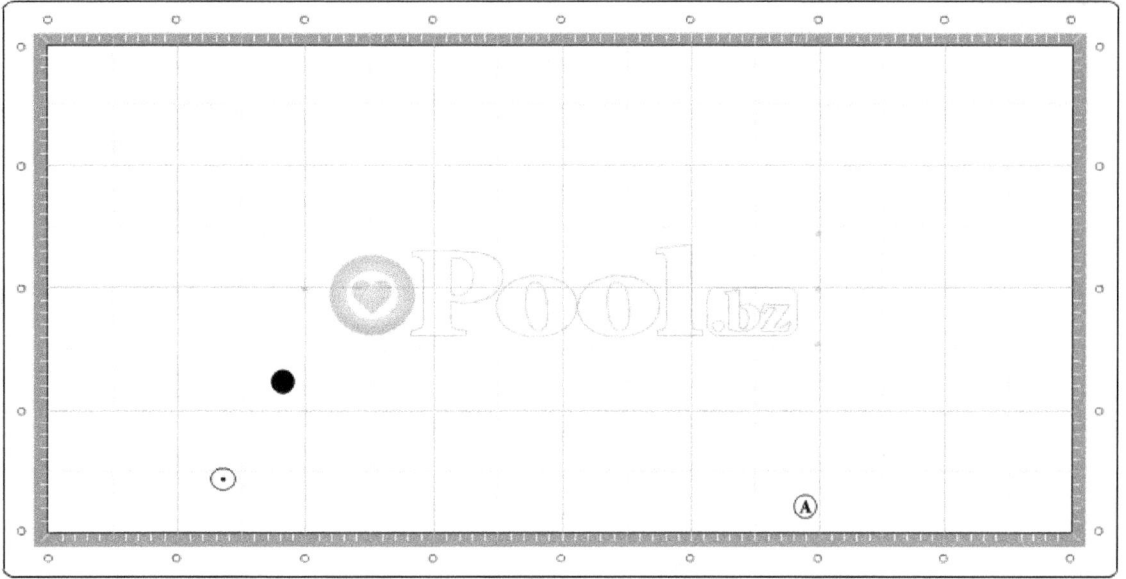

Shot Pattern

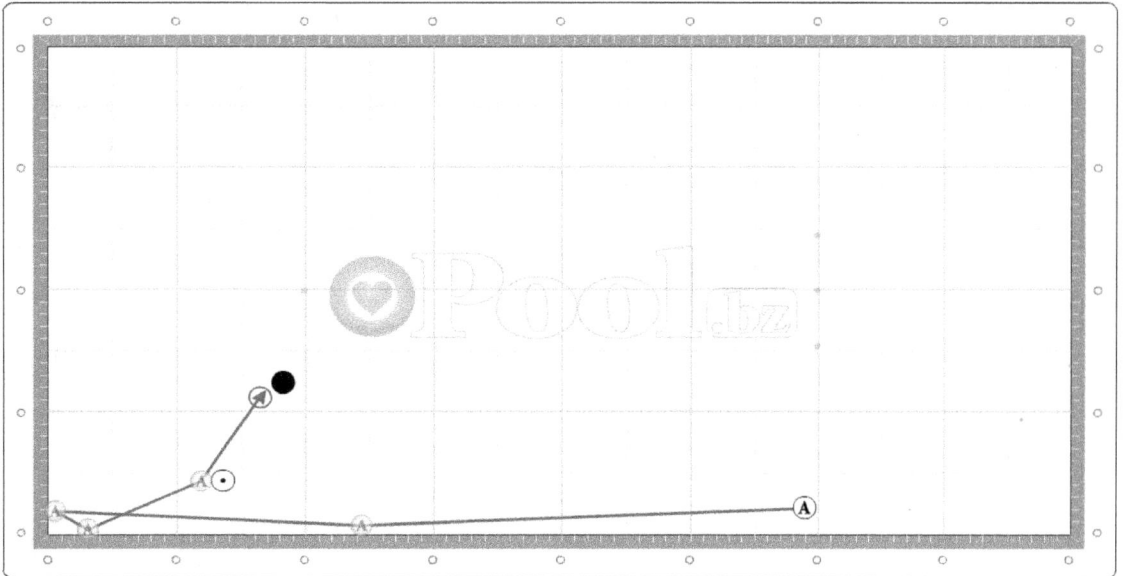

D:6b – Setup

Shot Pattern

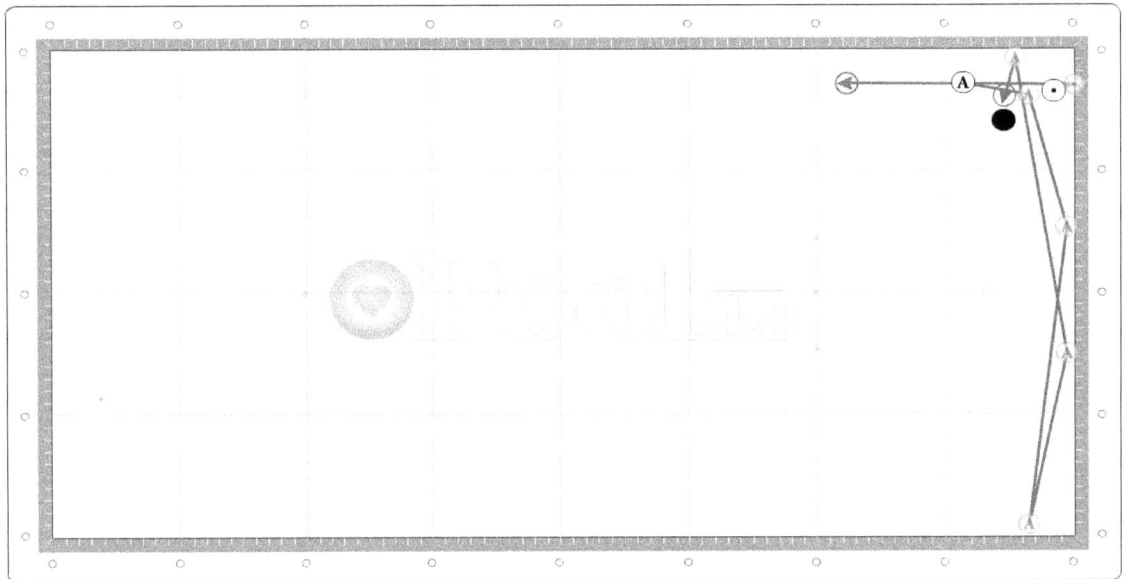

D:6c – Setup

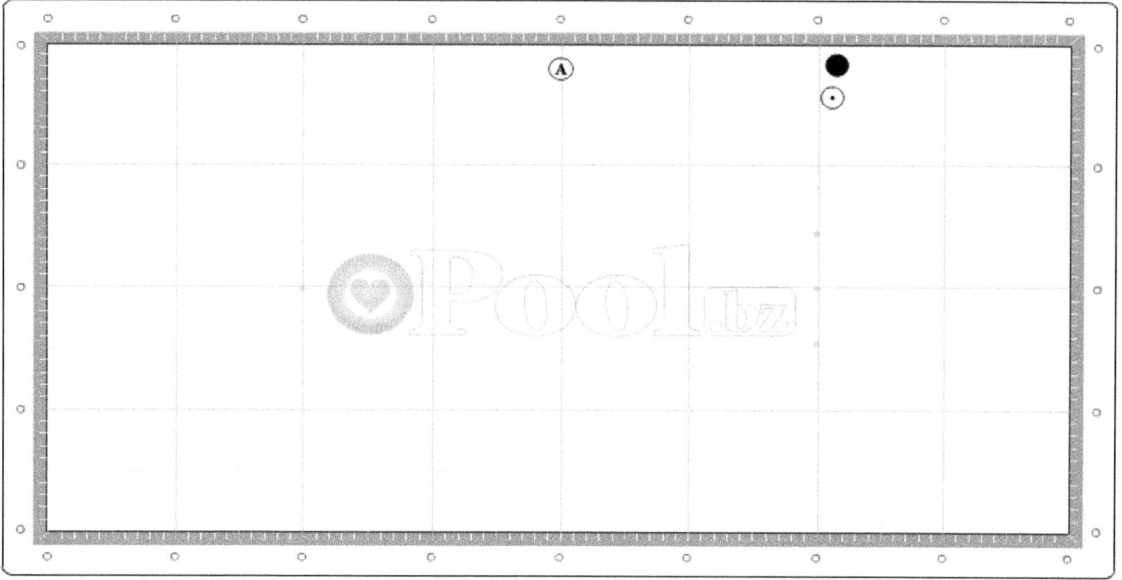

Shot Pattern

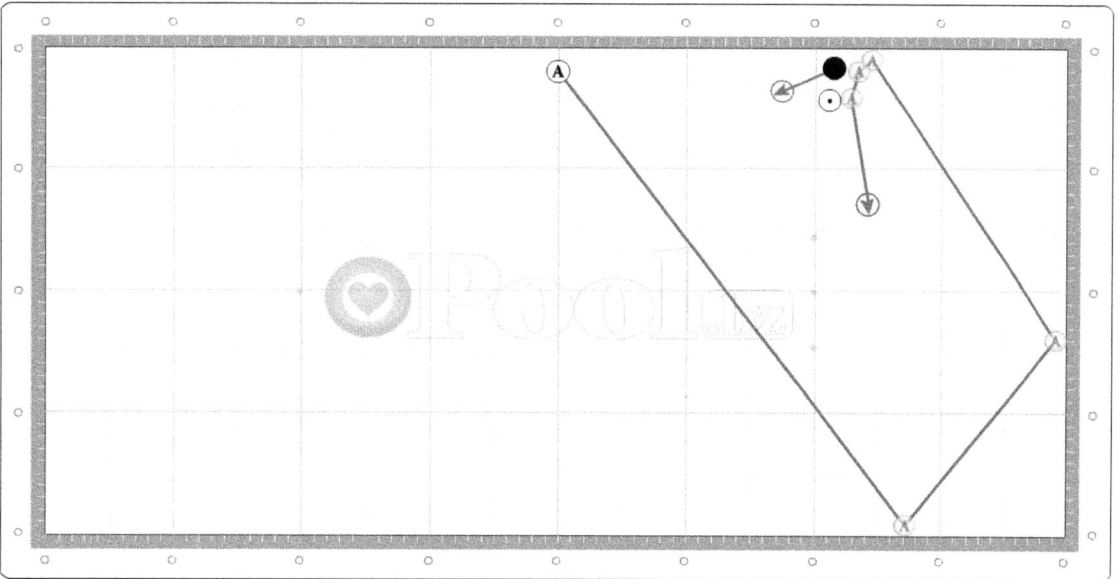

D:6d – Setup

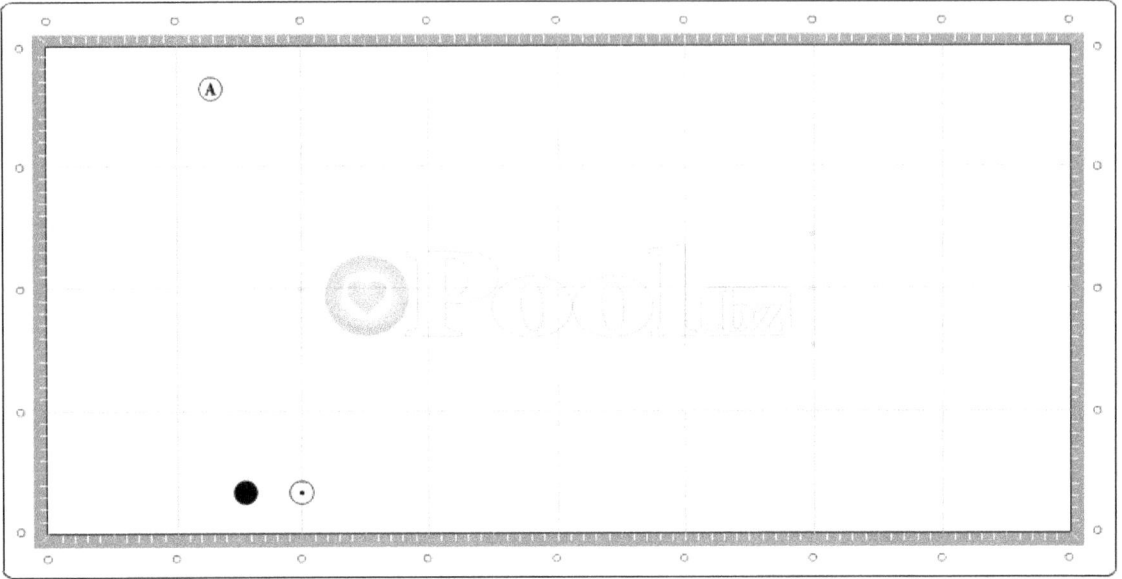

Shot Pattern

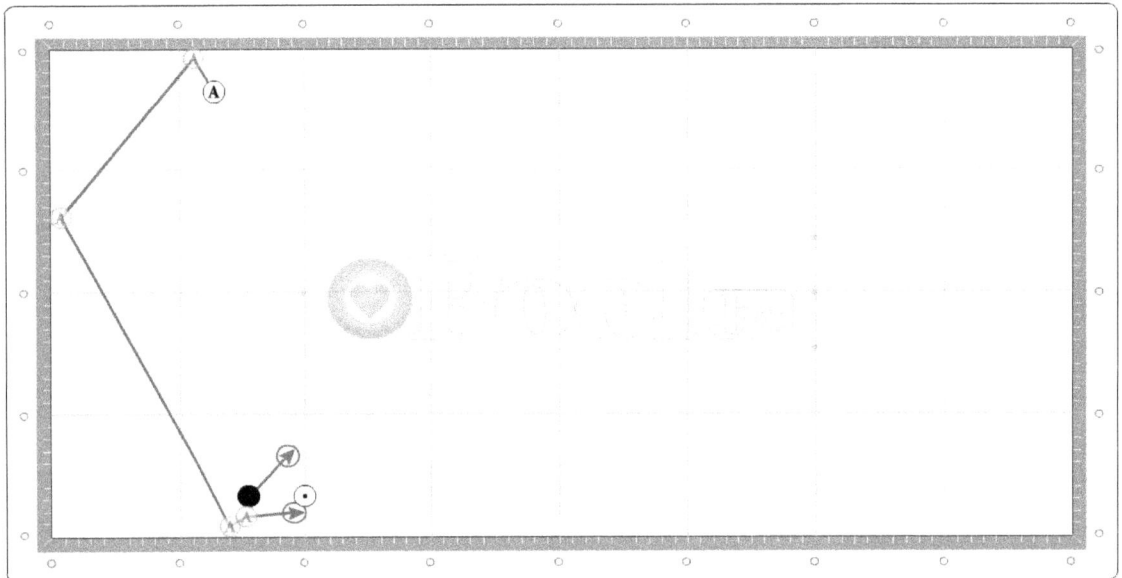

E: 3 cushions first, Series 2

Here are more 3-cushions first shots. As with section D, the CB goes into three rails before it contacts the first OB. Then the CB goes into the second OB for the point. Generally, the decision is based on the two OBs positioned close together.

E: Group 1

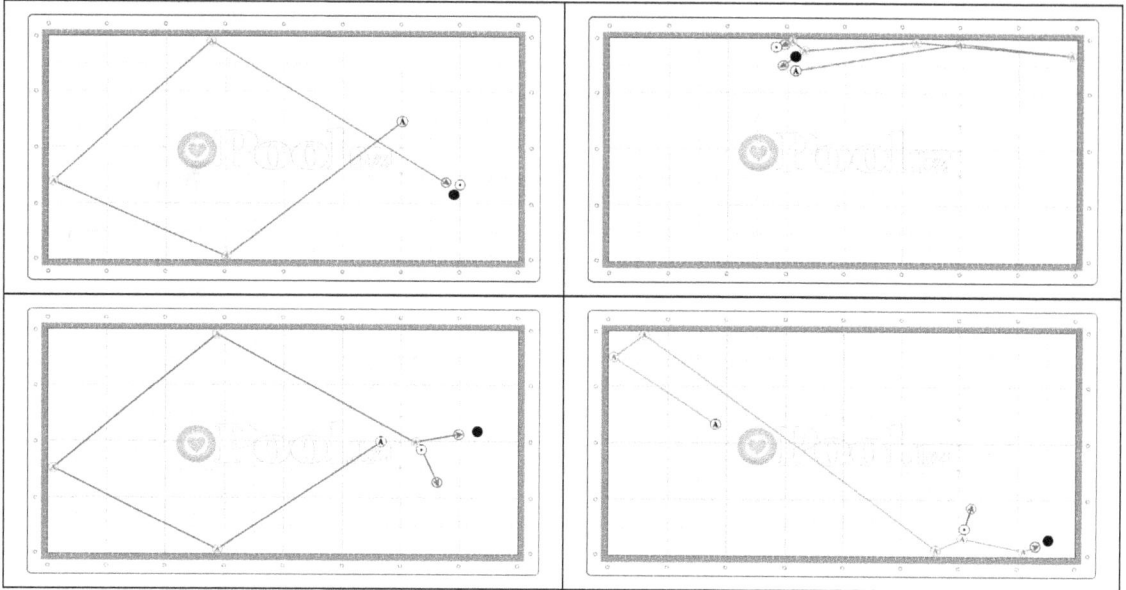

Analysis:

E:1a. _____

E:1b. _____

E:1c. _____

E:1d. _____

E:1a – Setup

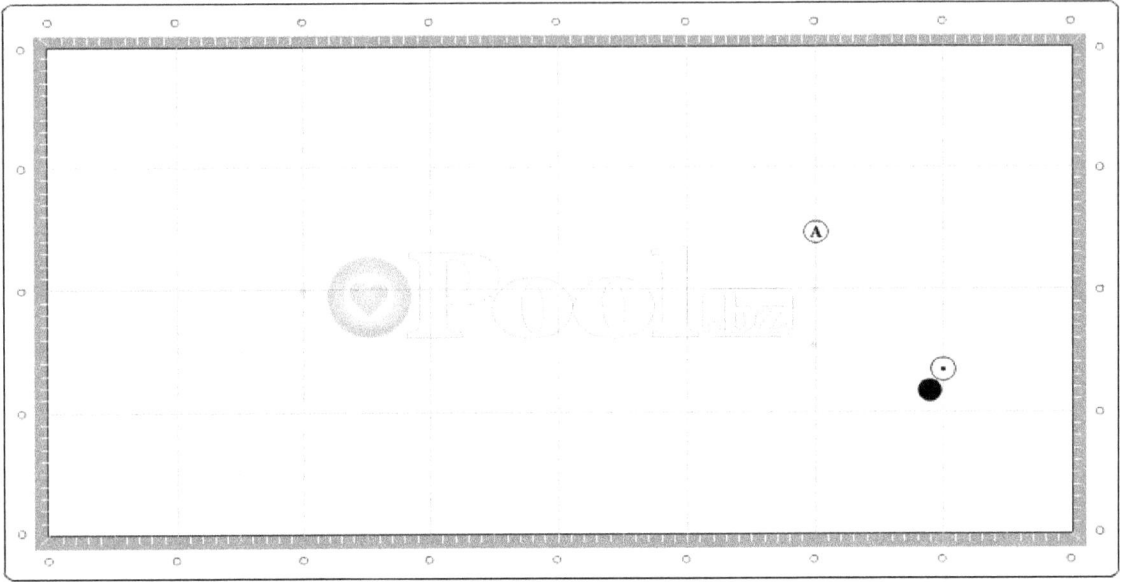

Shot Pattern

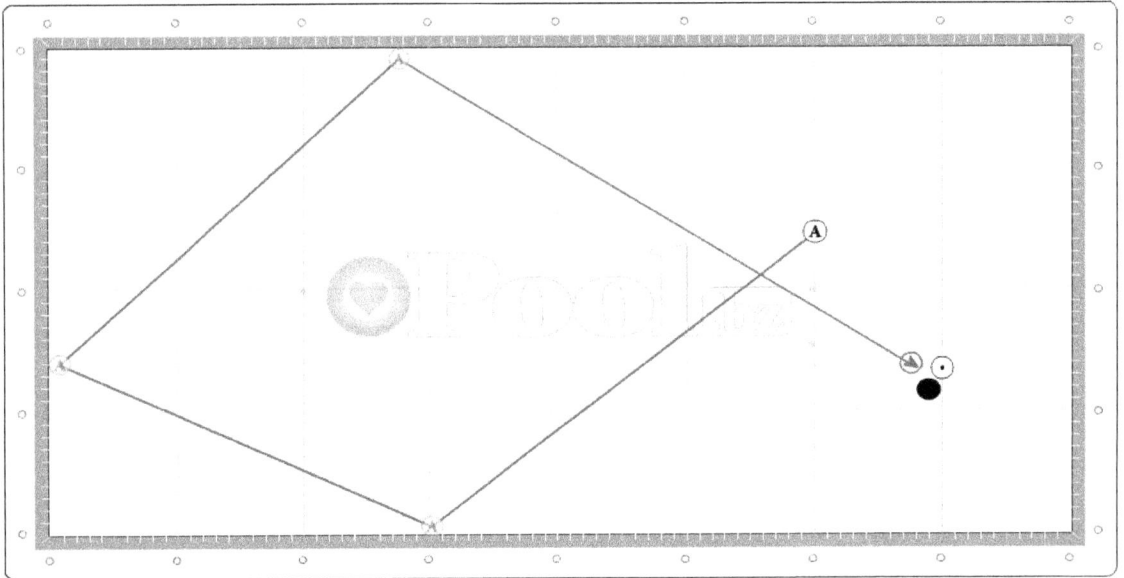

E:1b – Setup

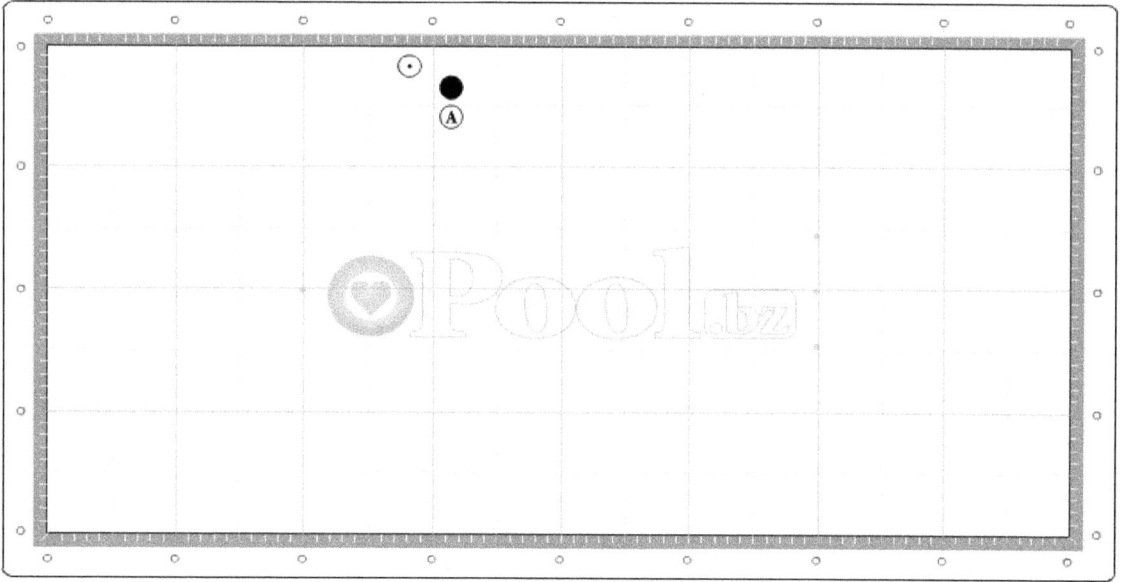

Shot Pattern

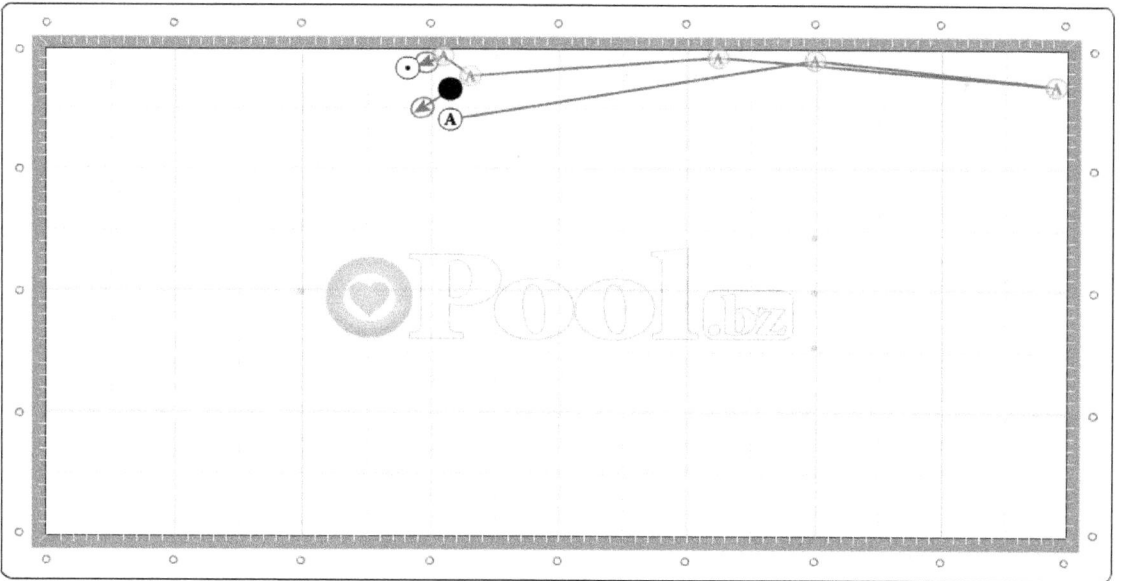

E:1c – Setup

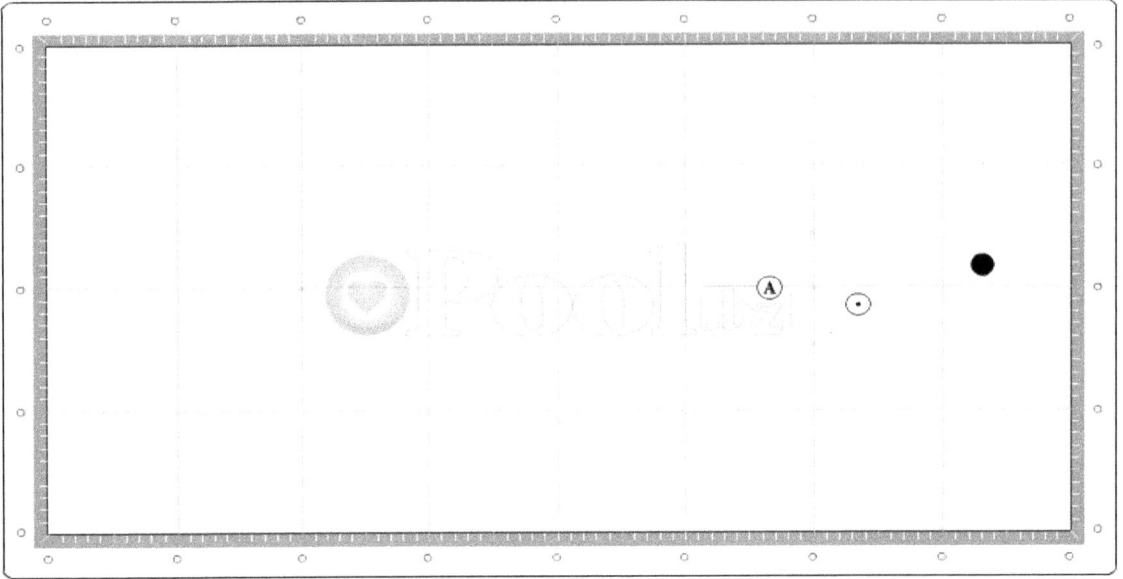

Shot Pattern

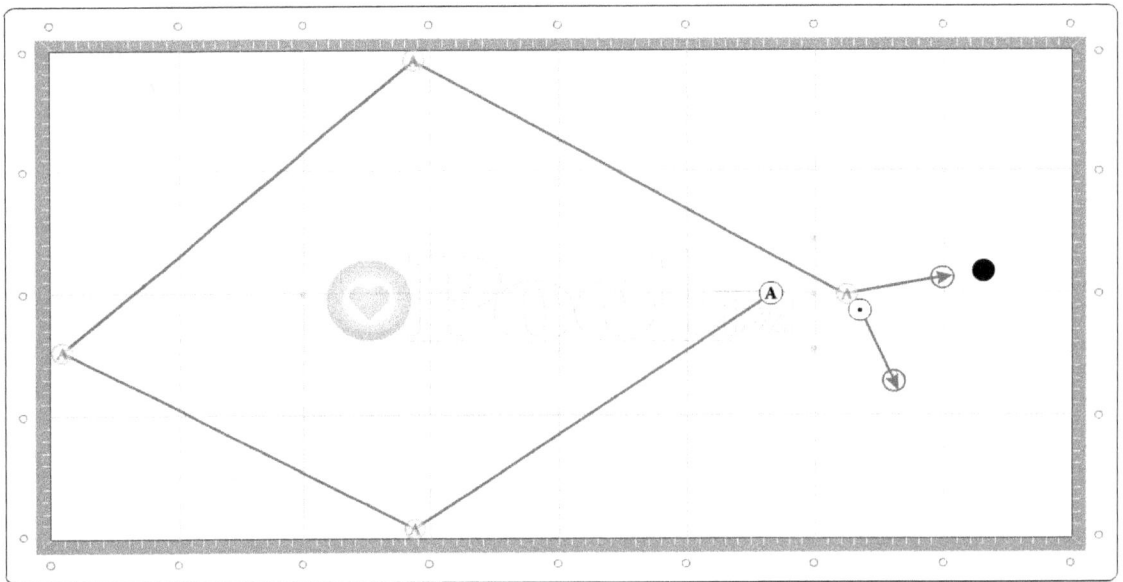

E:1d – Setup

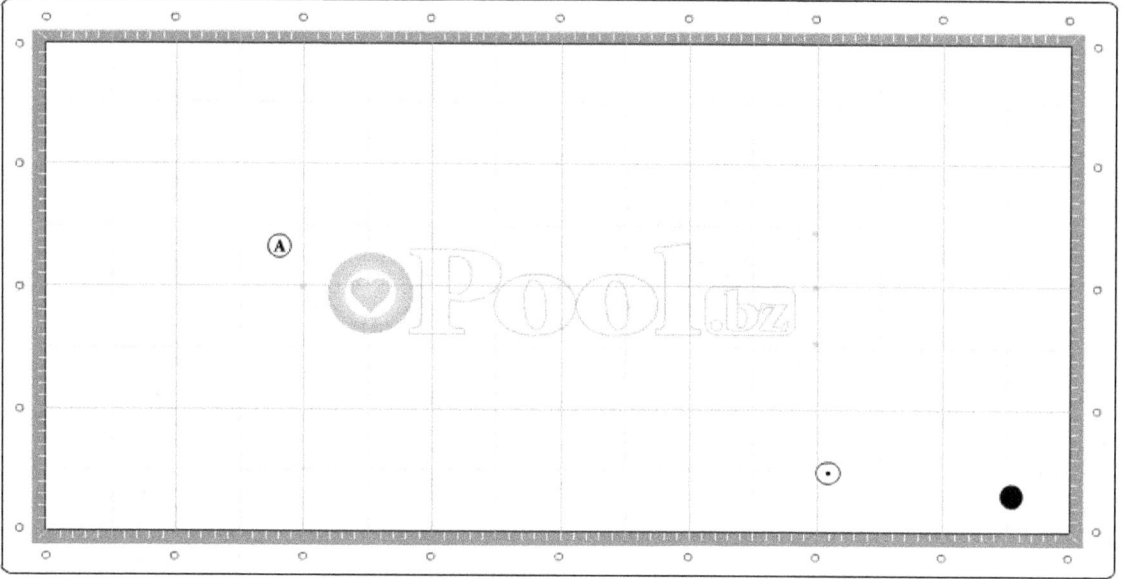

Shot Pattern

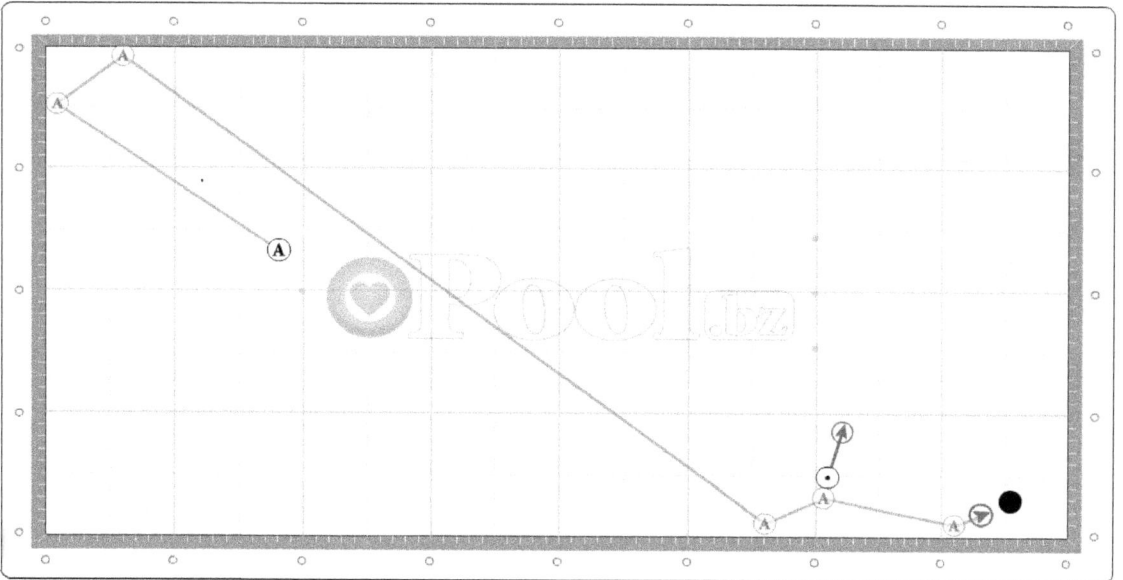

E: Group 2

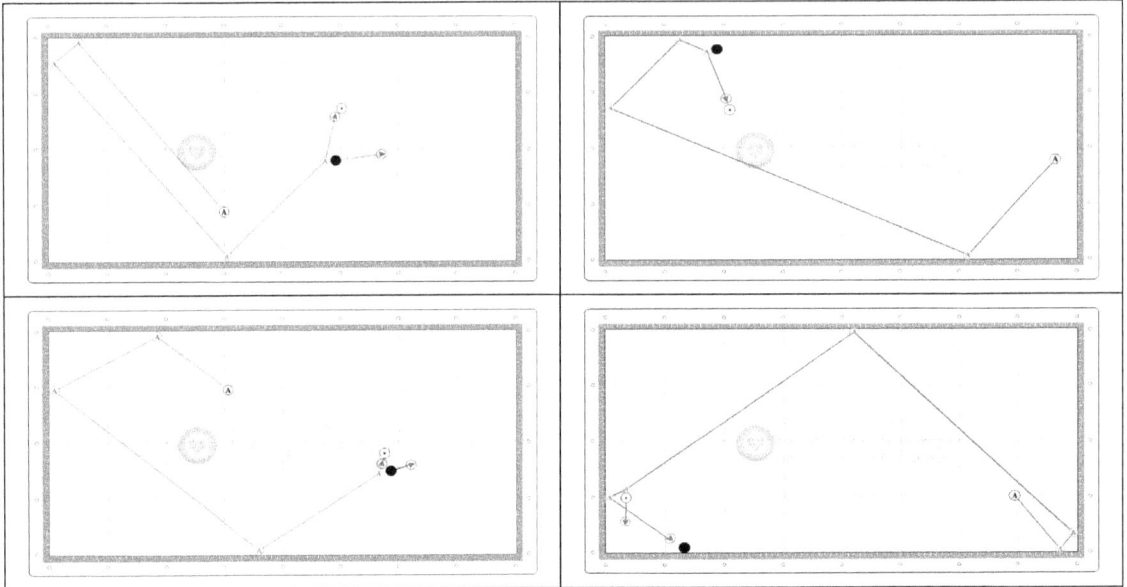

Analysis:

E:2a. _____

E:2b. _____

E:2c. _____

E:2d. _____

E:2a – Setup

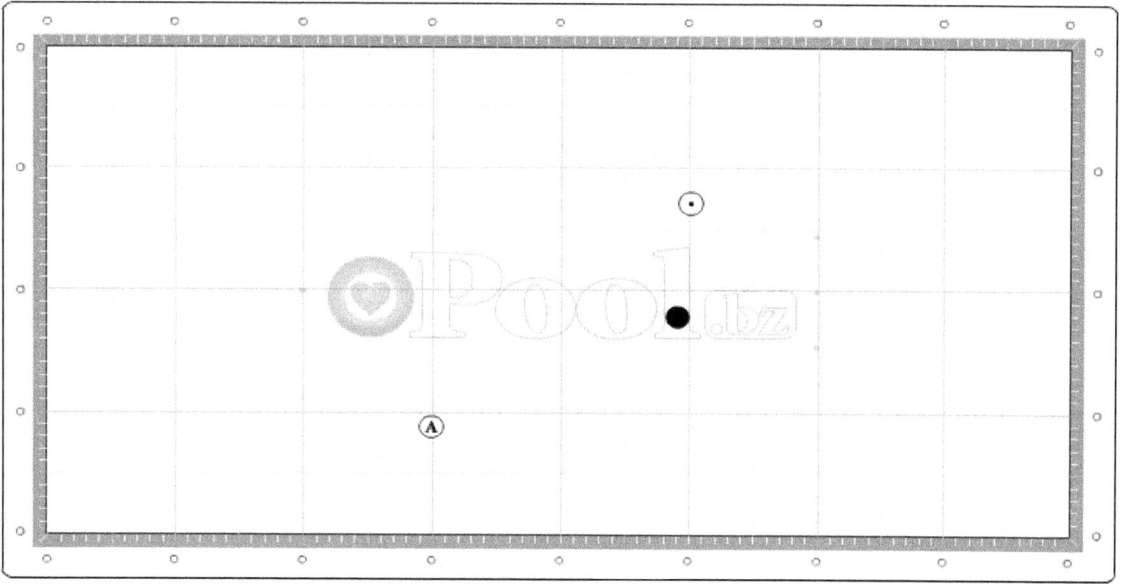

Shot Pattern

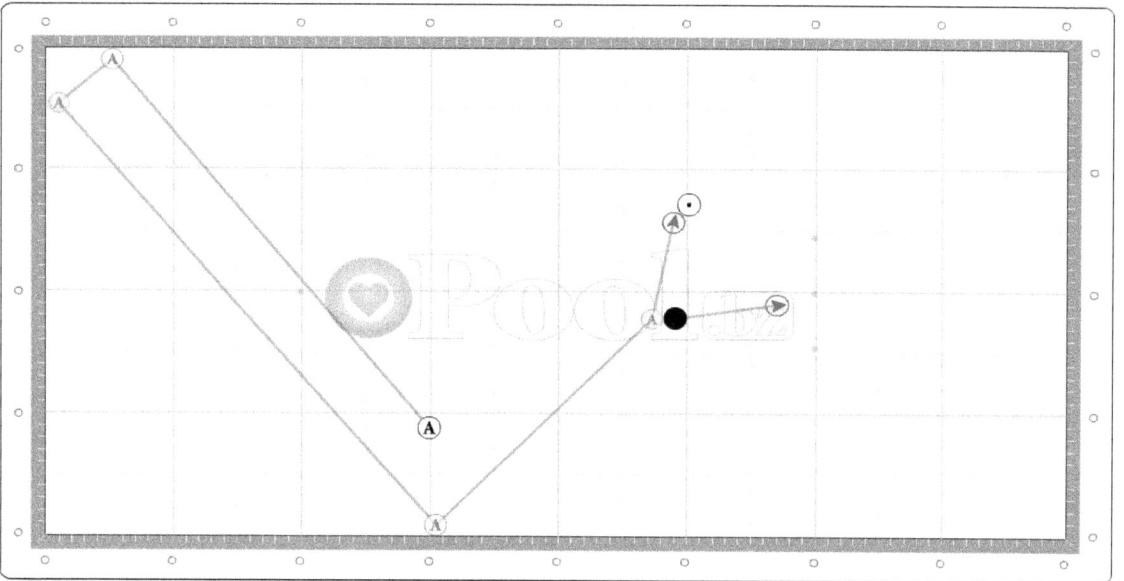

E:2b – Setup

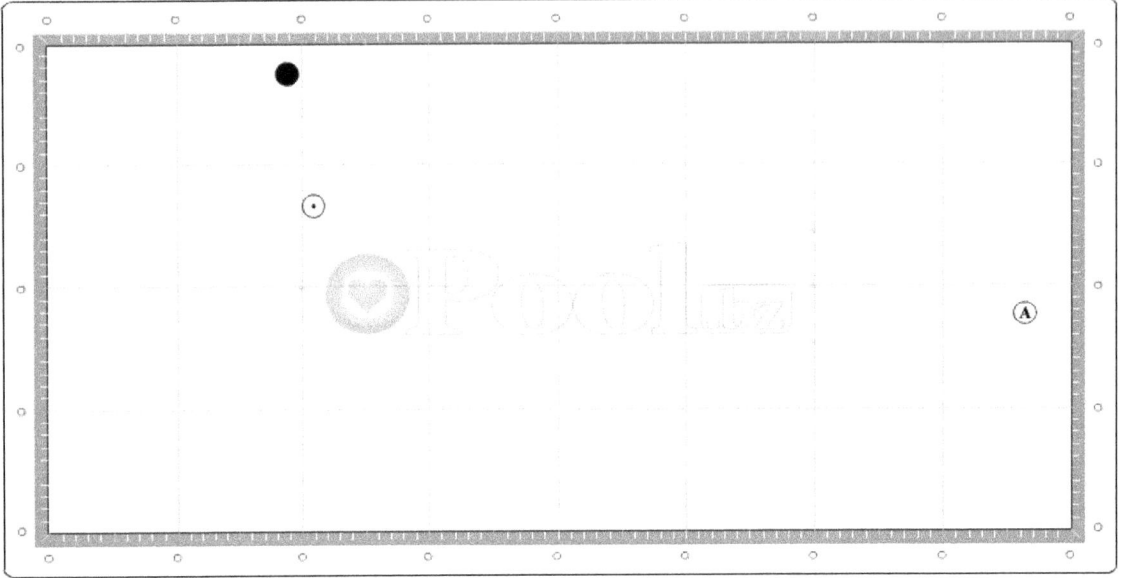

Shot Pattern

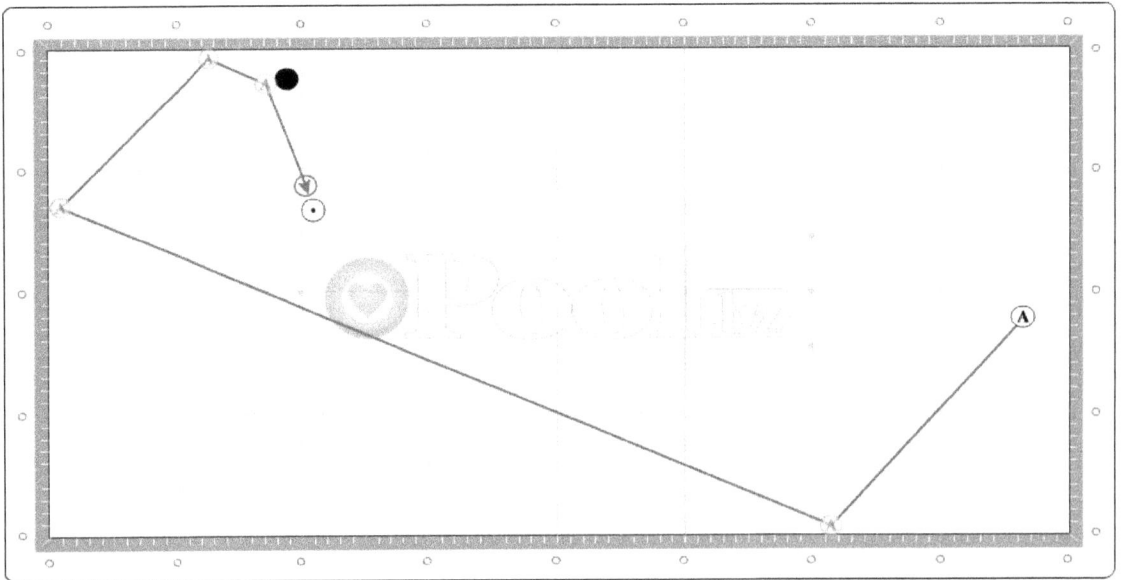

E:2c – Setup

Shot Pattern

E:2d – Setup

Shot Pattern

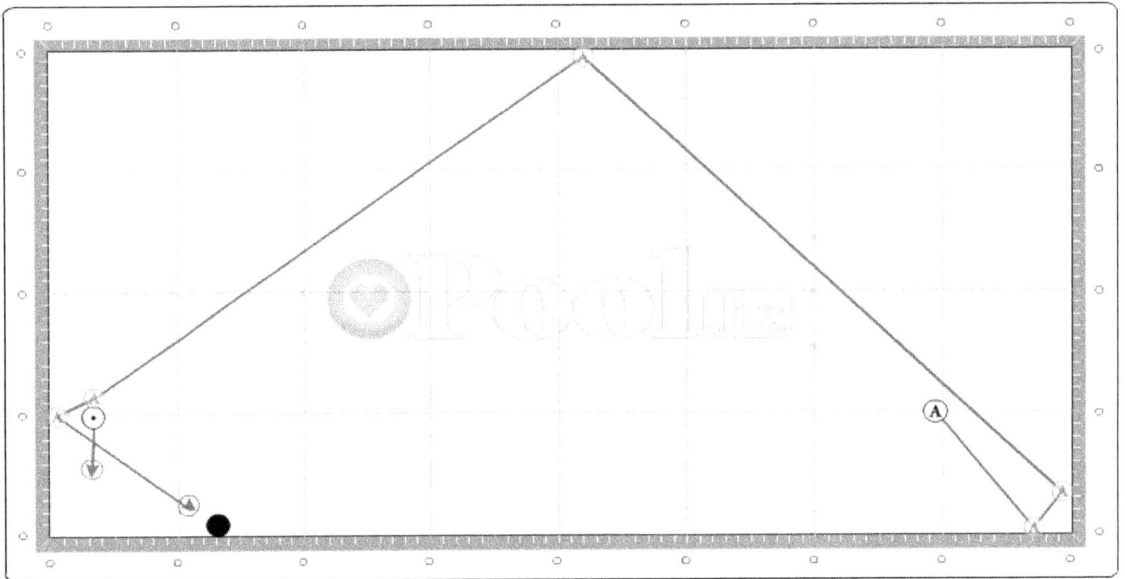

E: Group 3

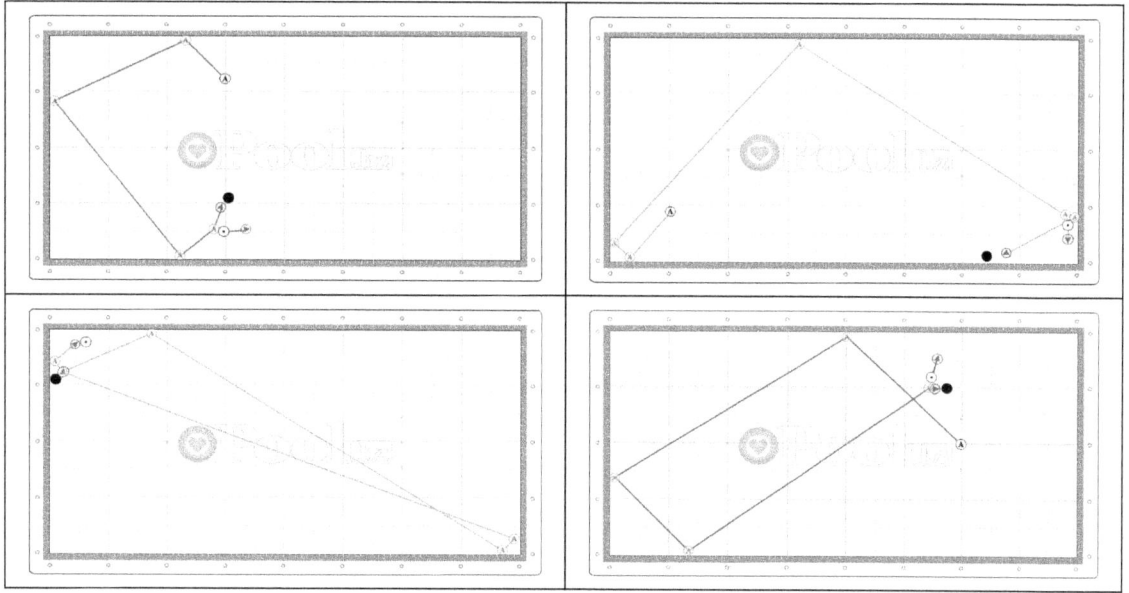

Analysis:

E:3a. _____

E:3b. _____

E:3c. _____

E:3d. _____

E:3a – Setup

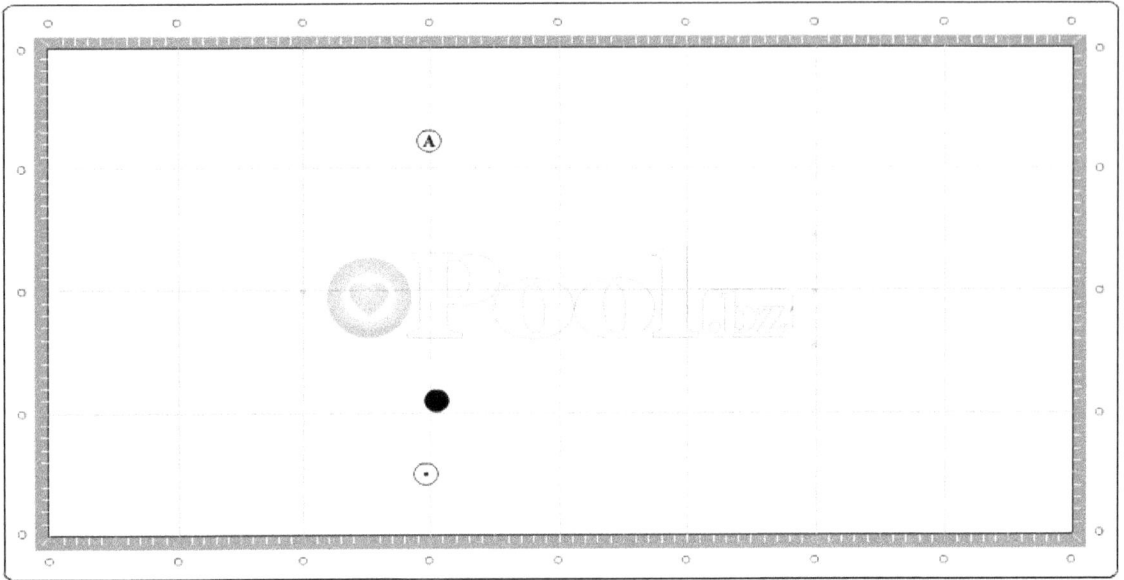

Shot Pattern

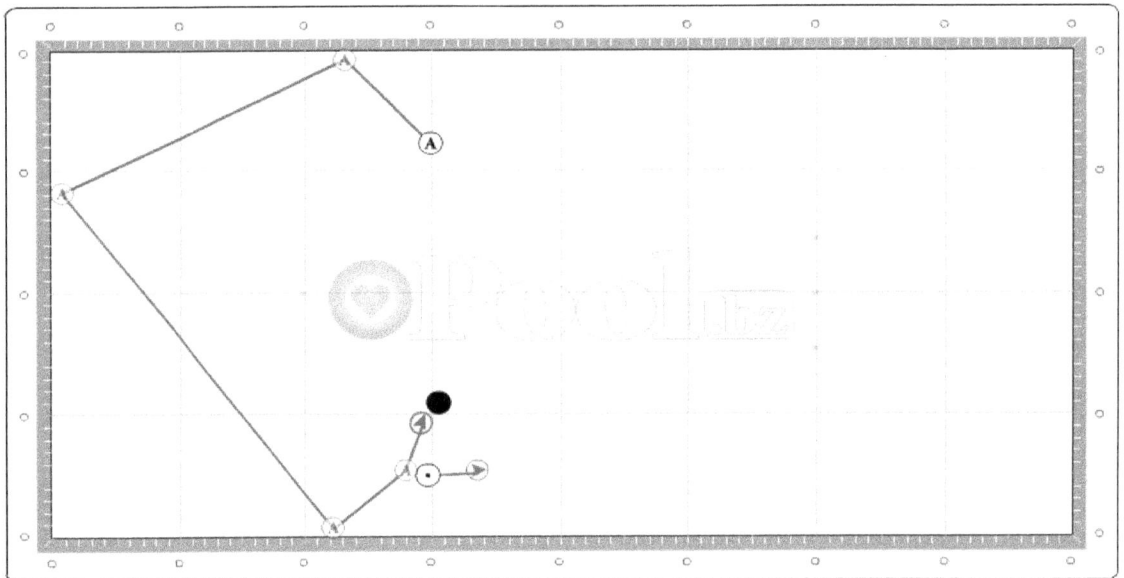

E:3b – Setup

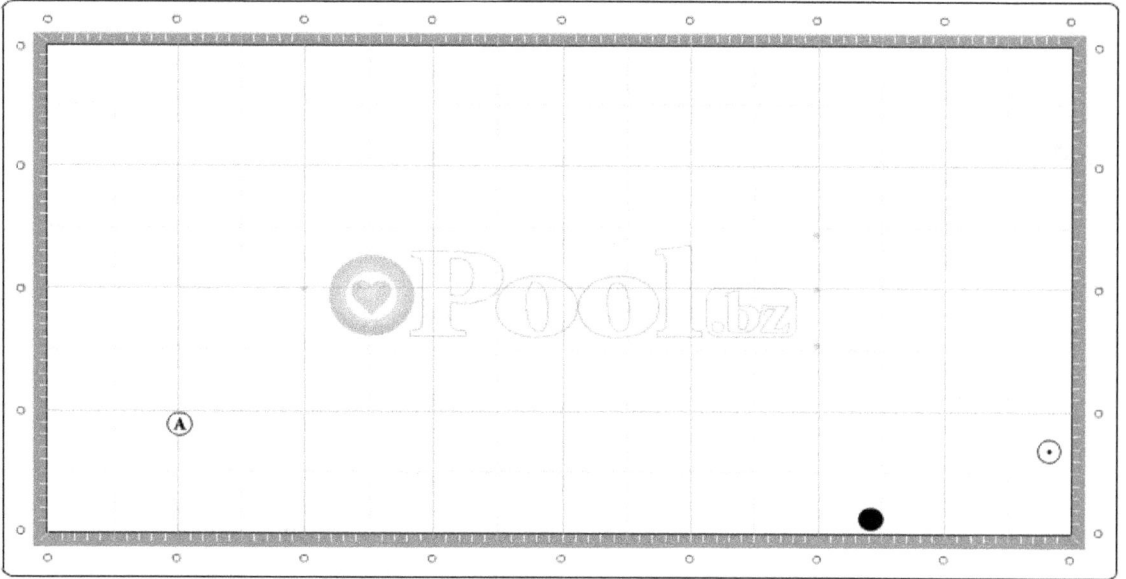

Shot Pattern

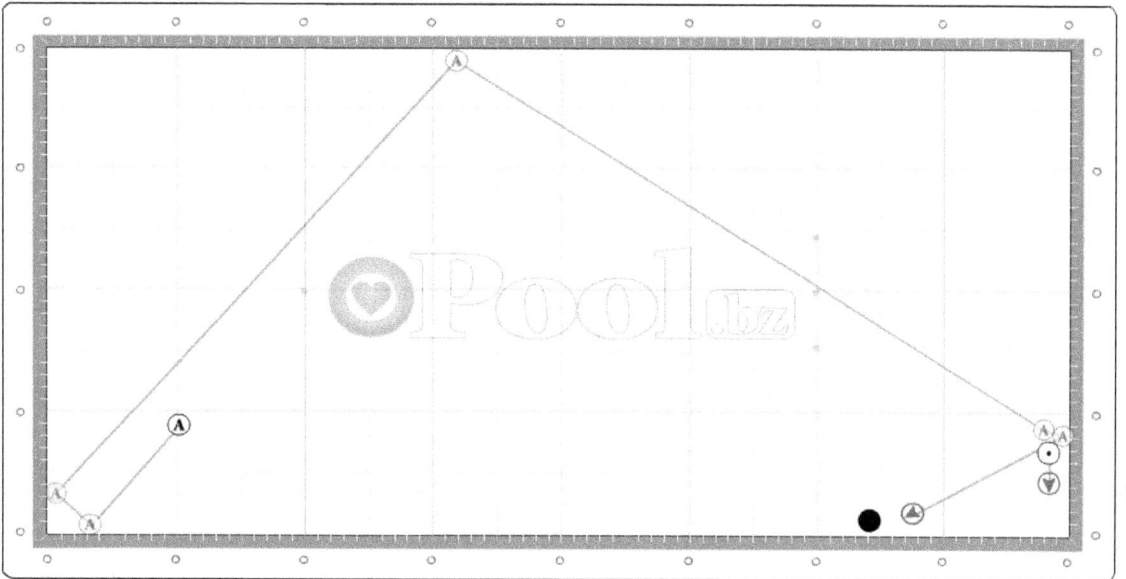

E:3c – Setup

Shot Pattern

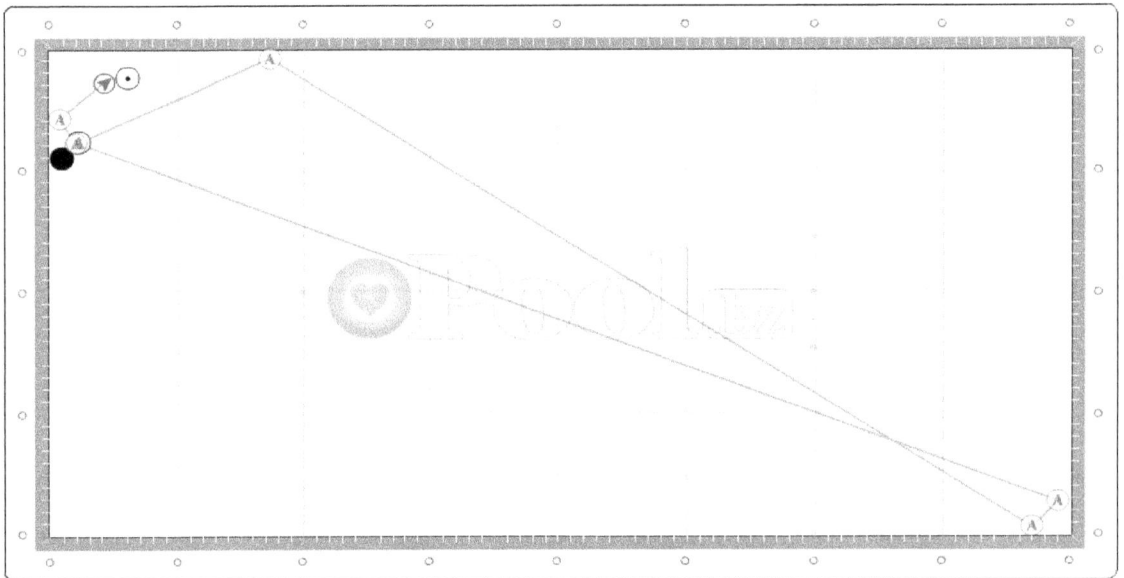

E:3d – Setup

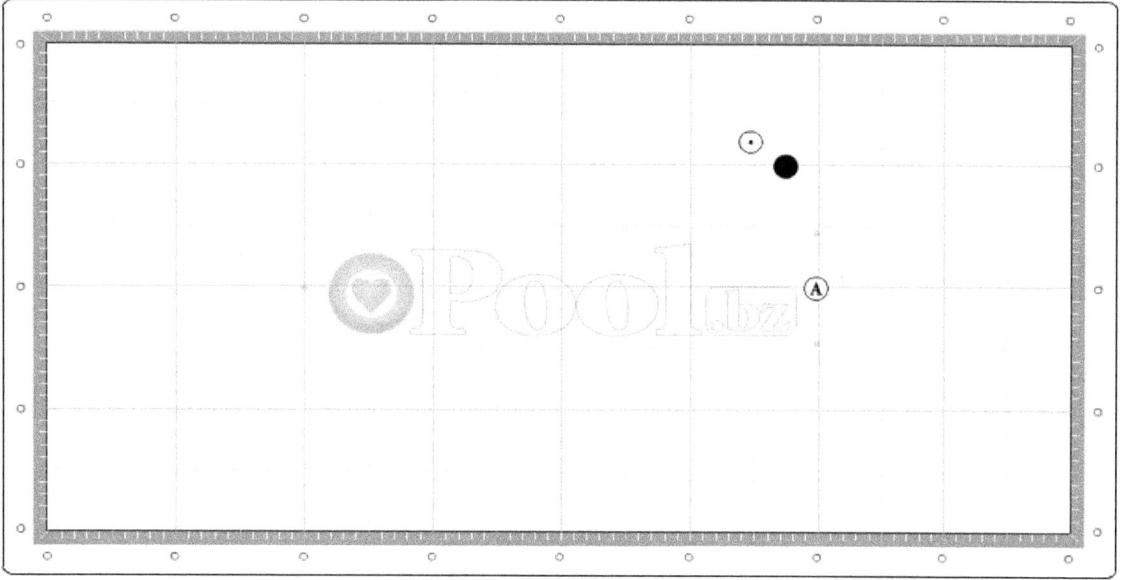

Shot Pattern

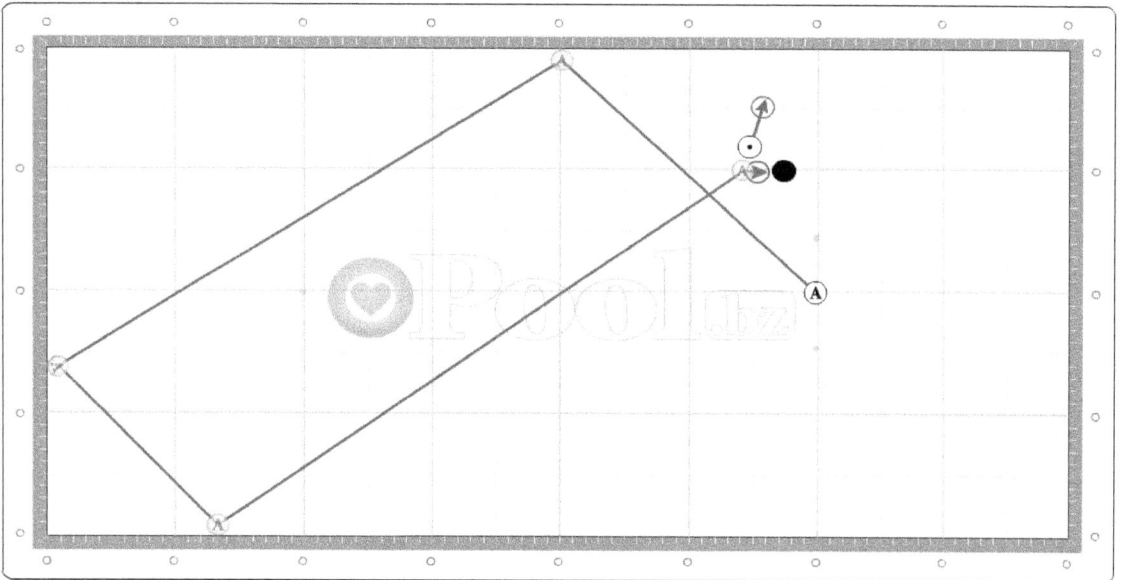

E: Group 4

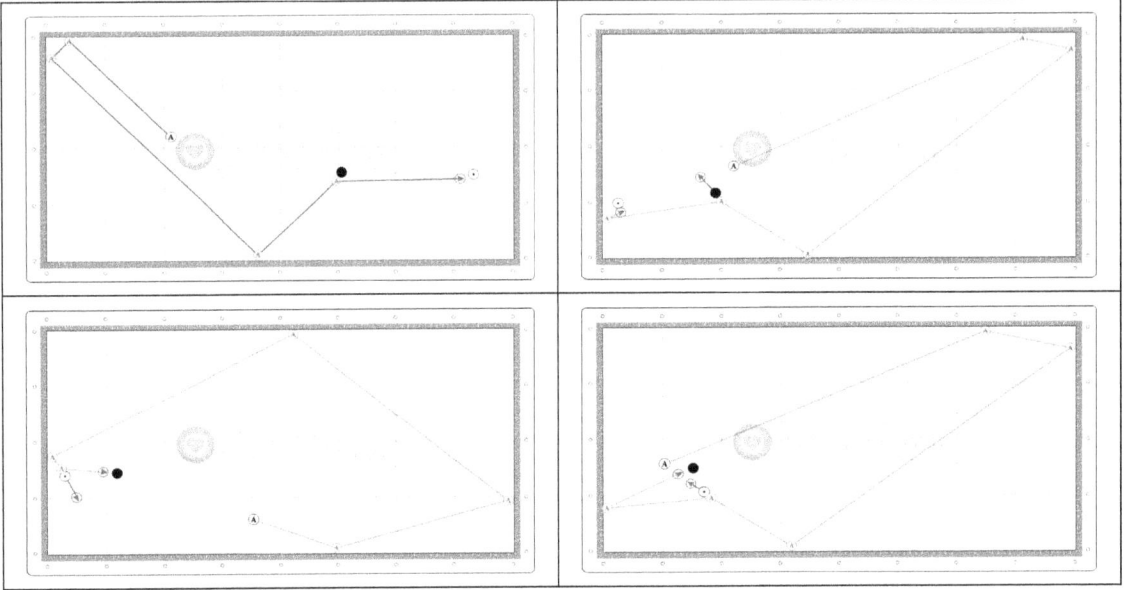

Analysis:

E:4a. _____

E:4b._____

E:4c. _____

E:4d. _____

E:4a – Setup

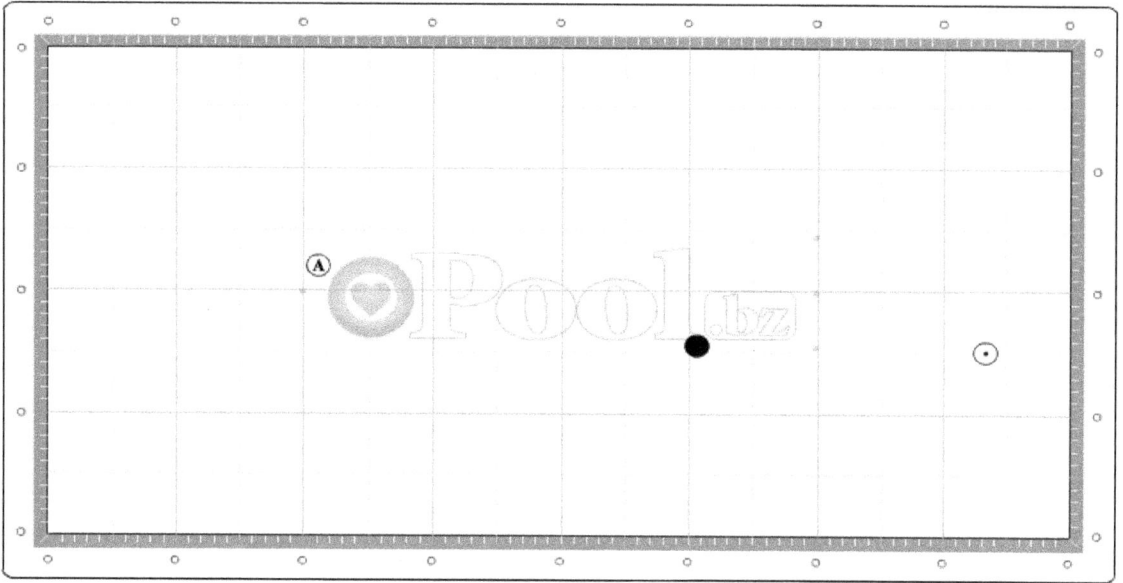

Shot Pattern

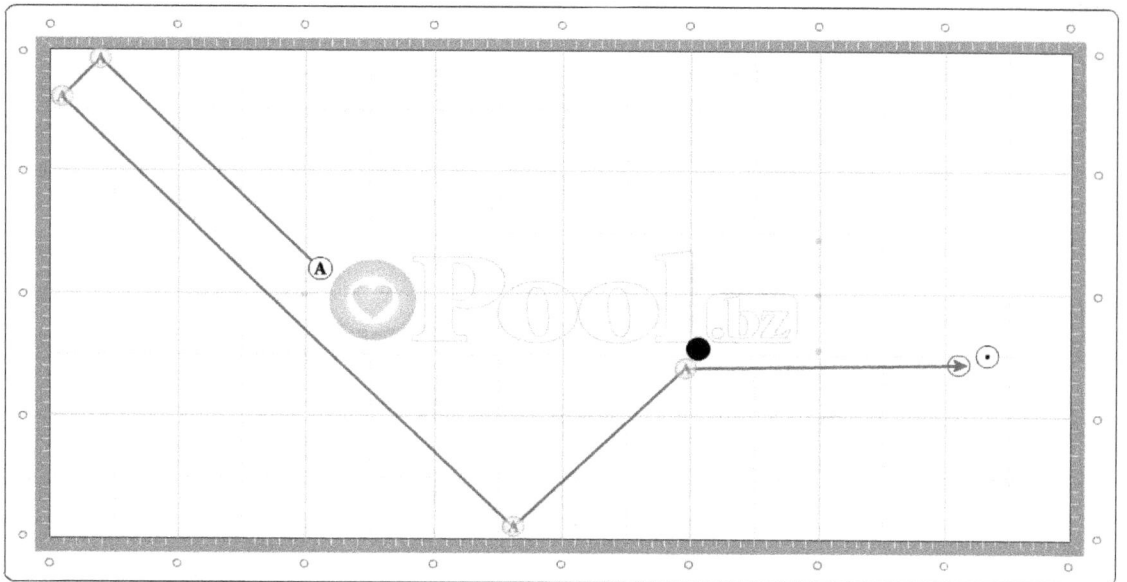

E:4b – Setup

Shot Pattern

E:4c – Setup

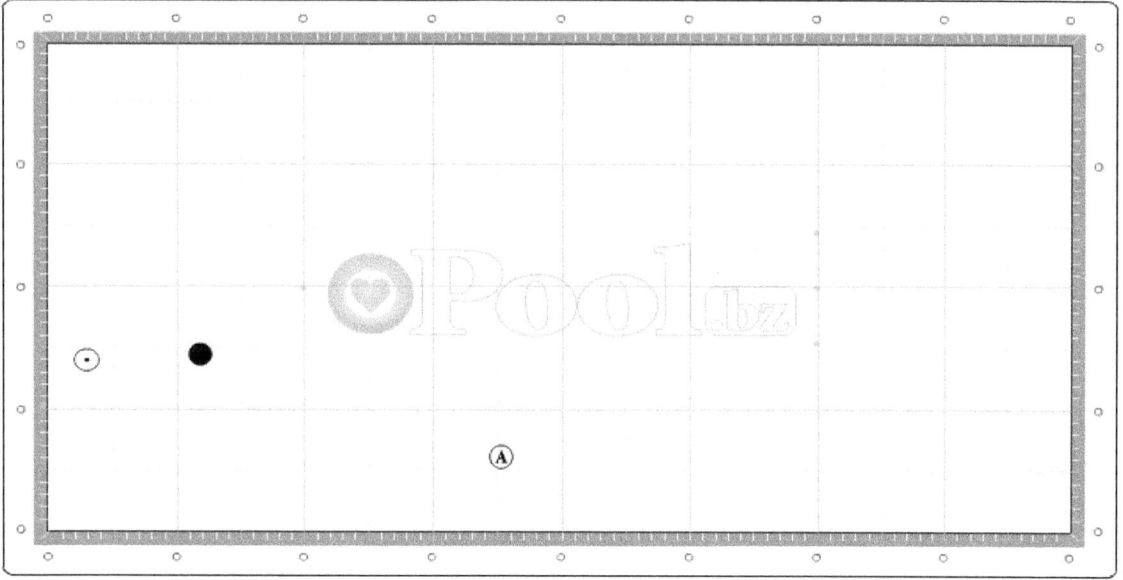

Shot Pattern

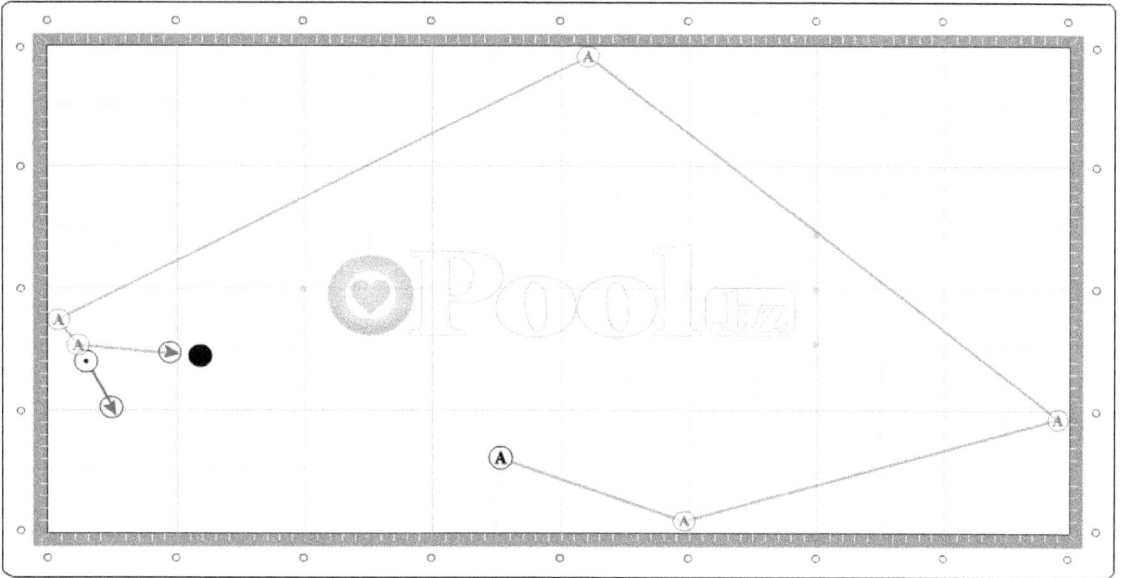

E:4d – Setup

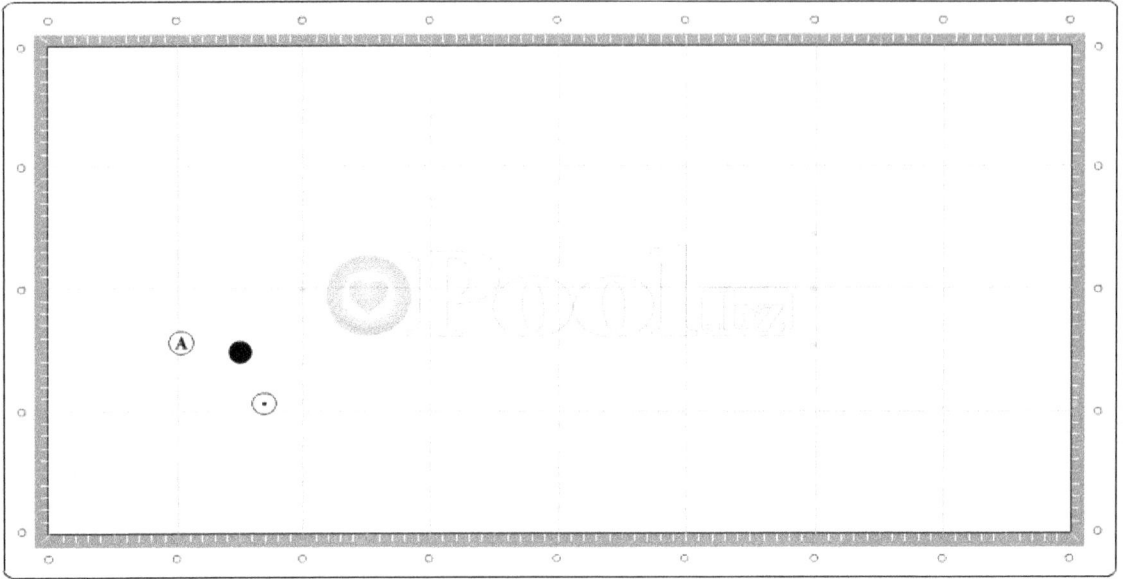

Shot Pattern

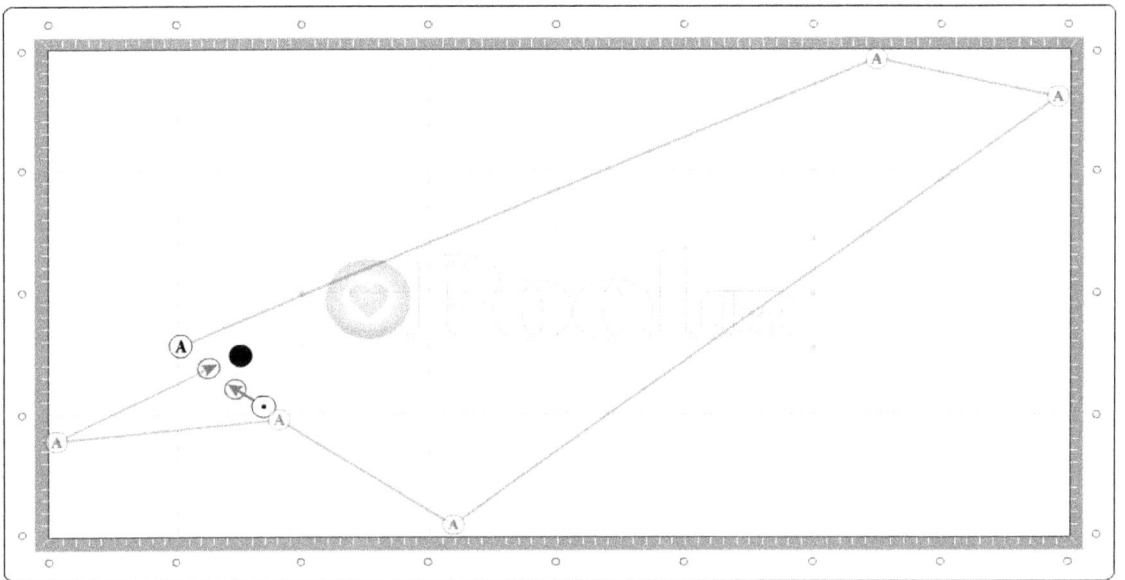

E: Group 5

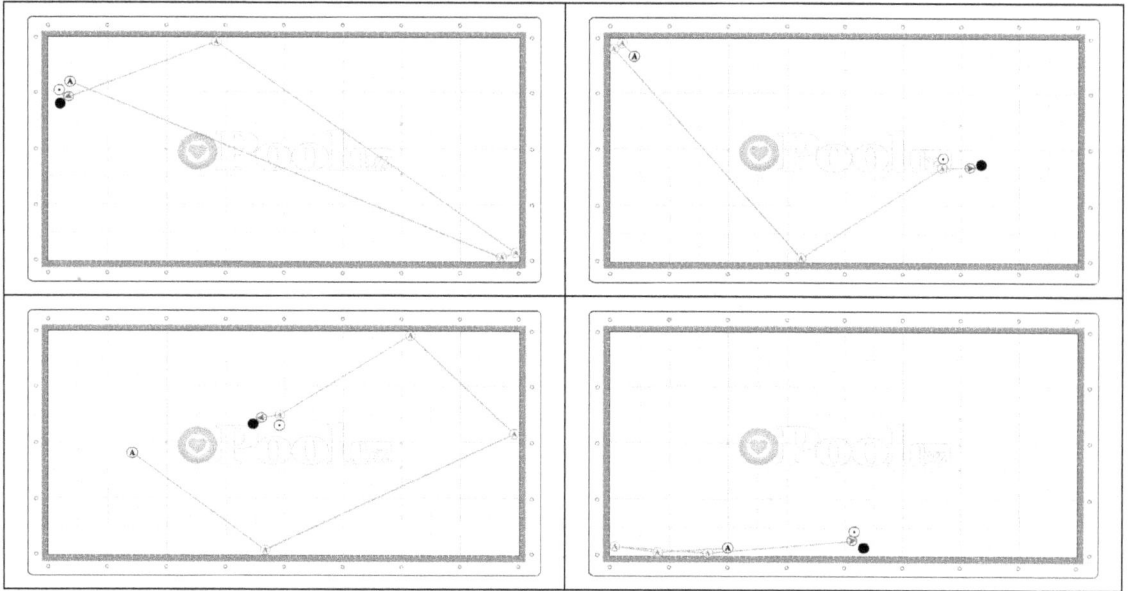

Analysis:

E:5a. _____

E:5b. _____

E:5c. _____

E:5d. _____

E:5a – Setup

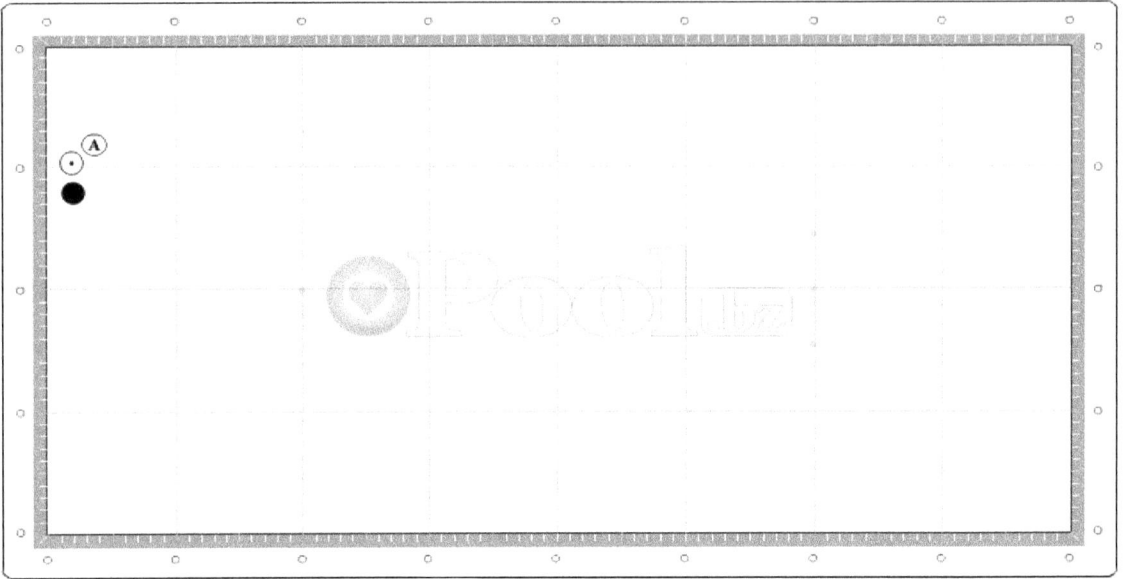

Shot Pattern

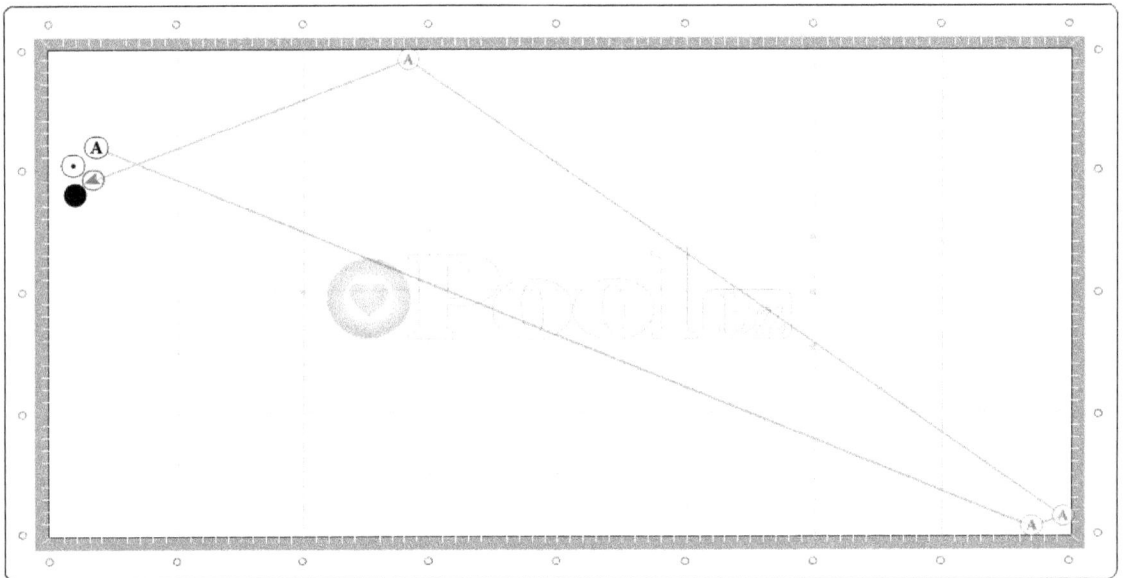

E:5b – Setup

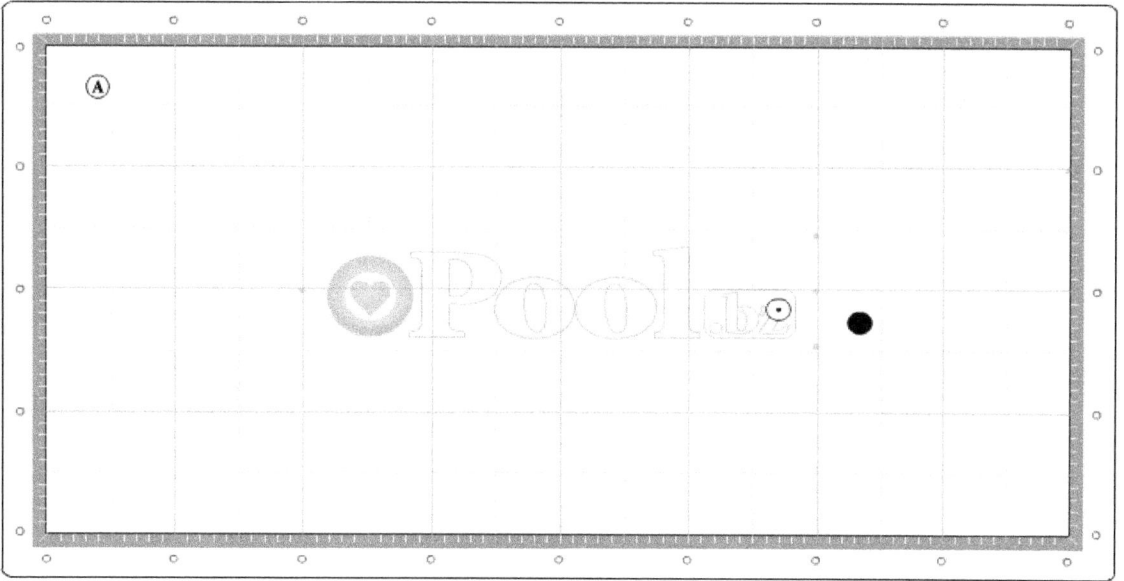

Shot Pattern

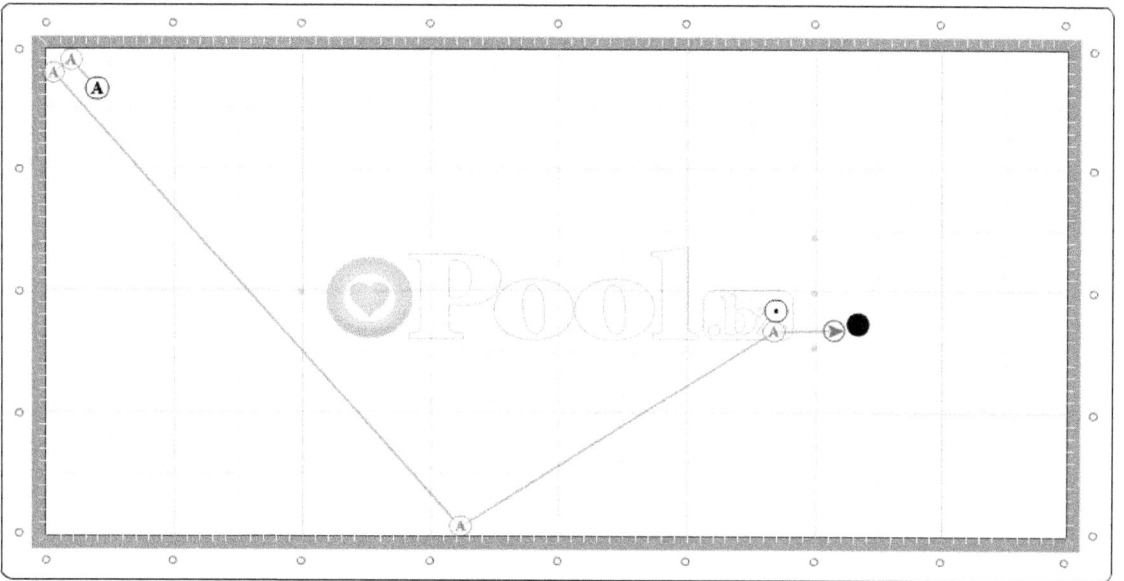

E:5c – Setup

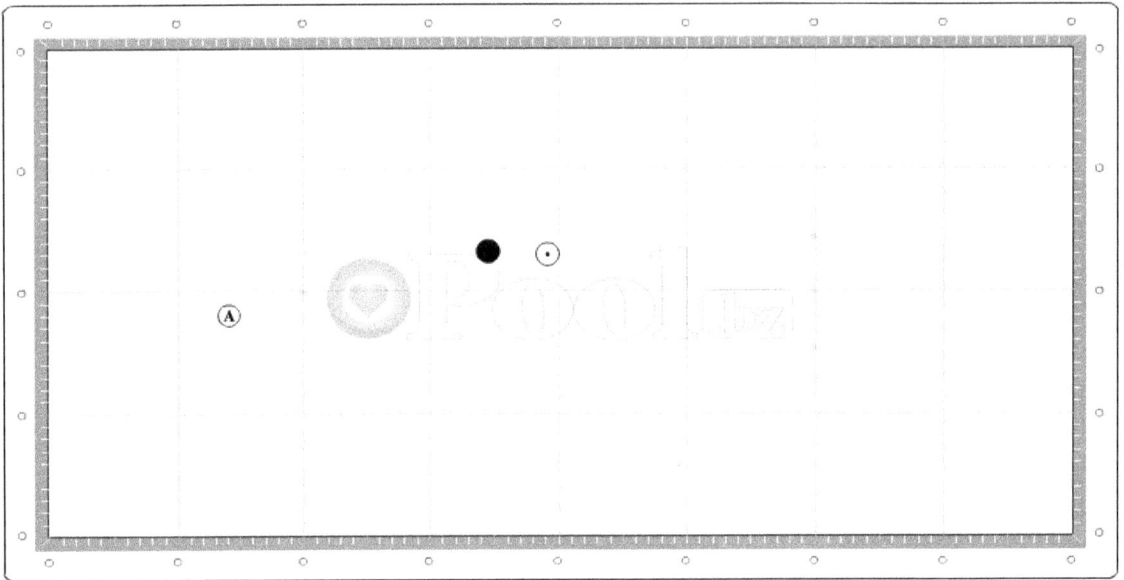

Shot Pattern

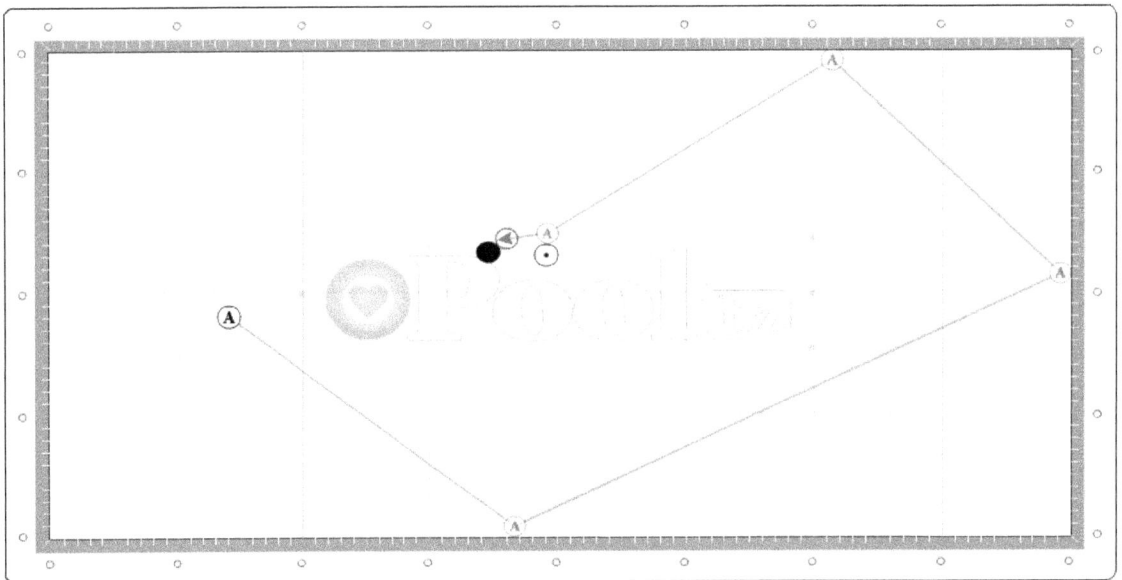

E:5d – Setup

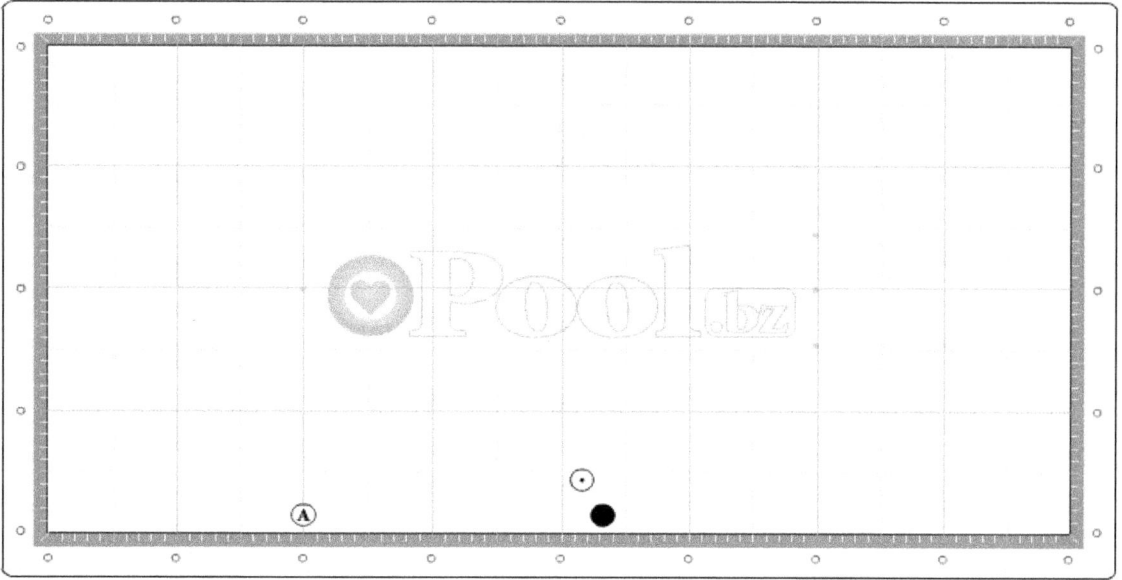

Shot Pattern

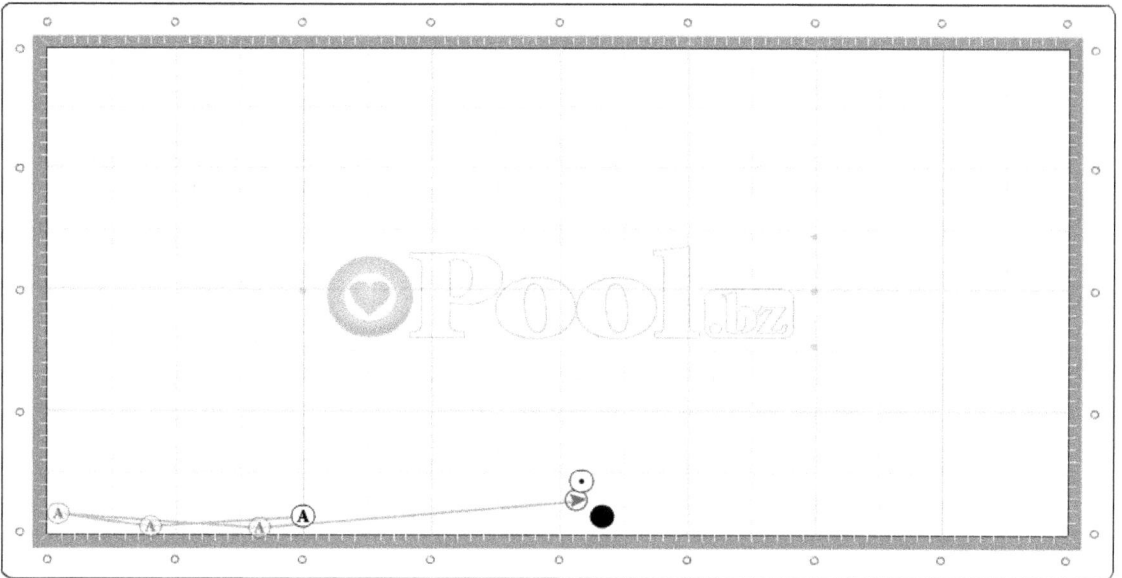

E: Group 6

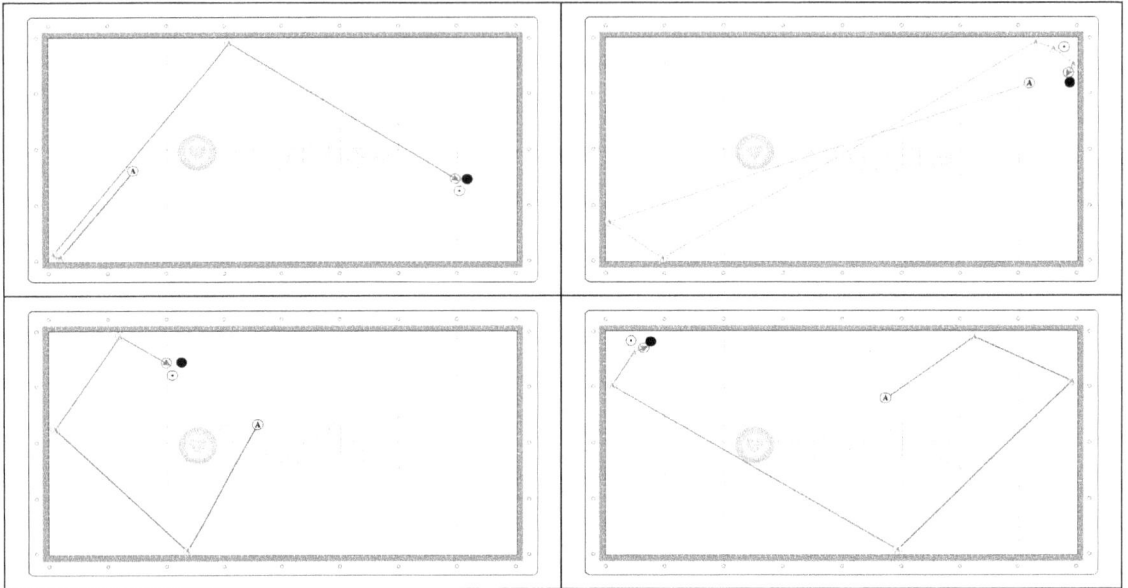

Analysis:

E:6a. _____

E:6b. _____

E:6c. _____

E:6d. _____

E:6a – Setup

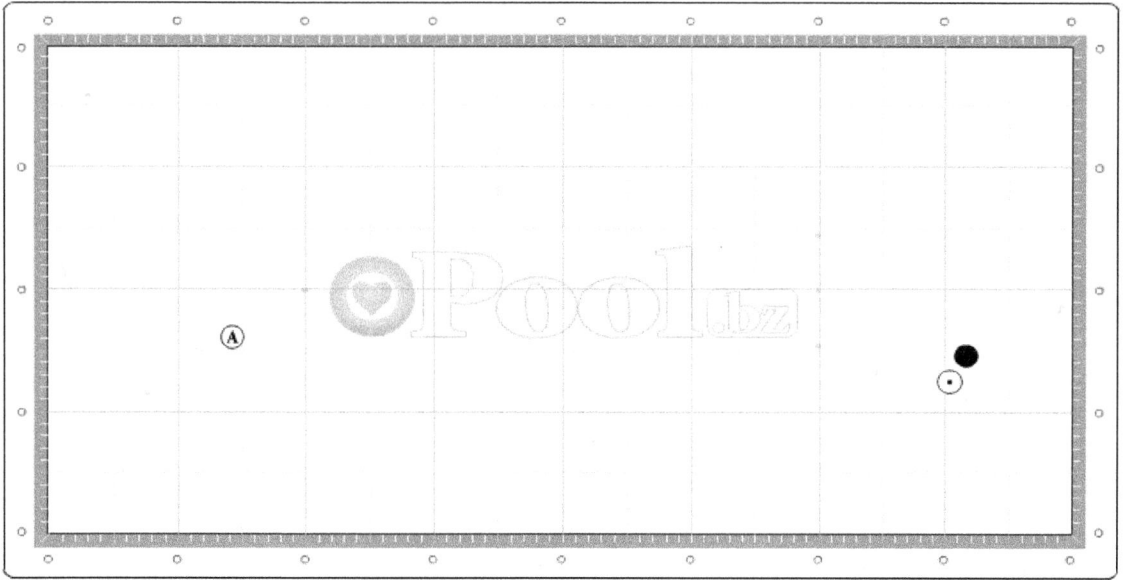

Shot Pattern

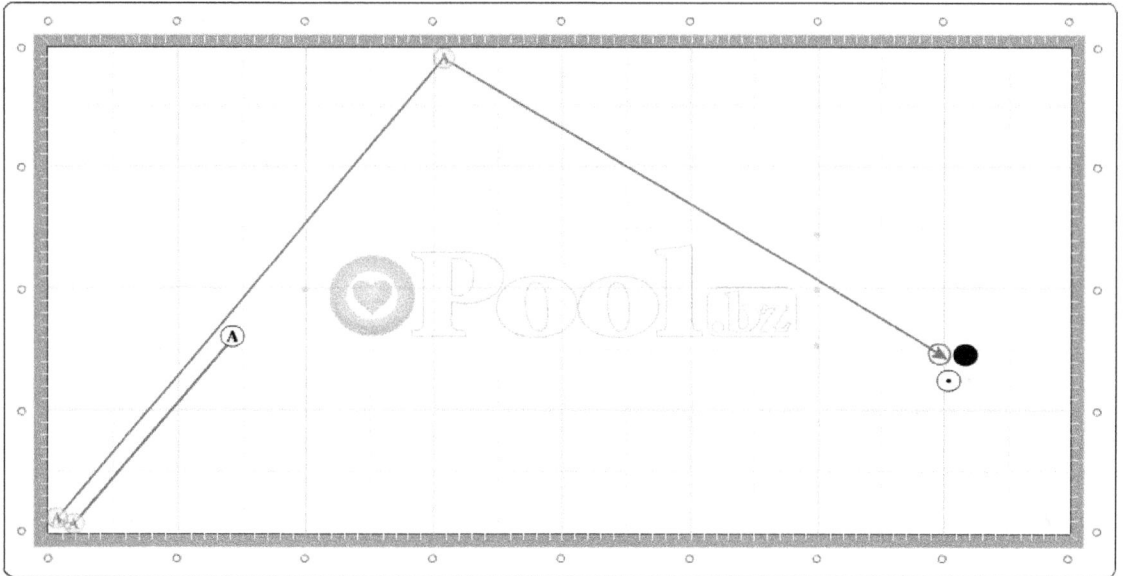

E:6b – Setup

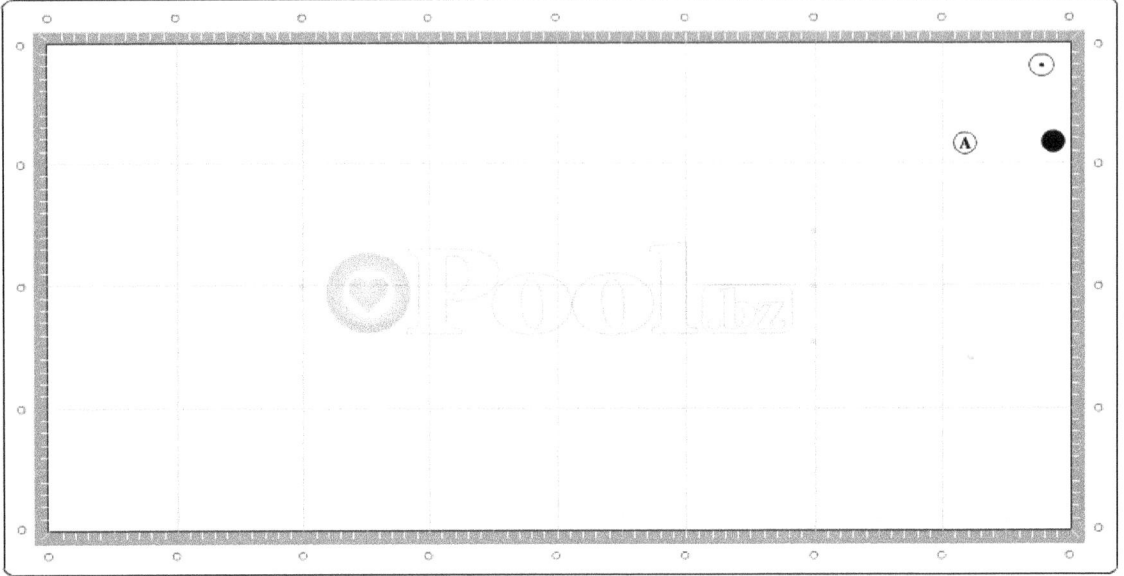

Shot Pattern

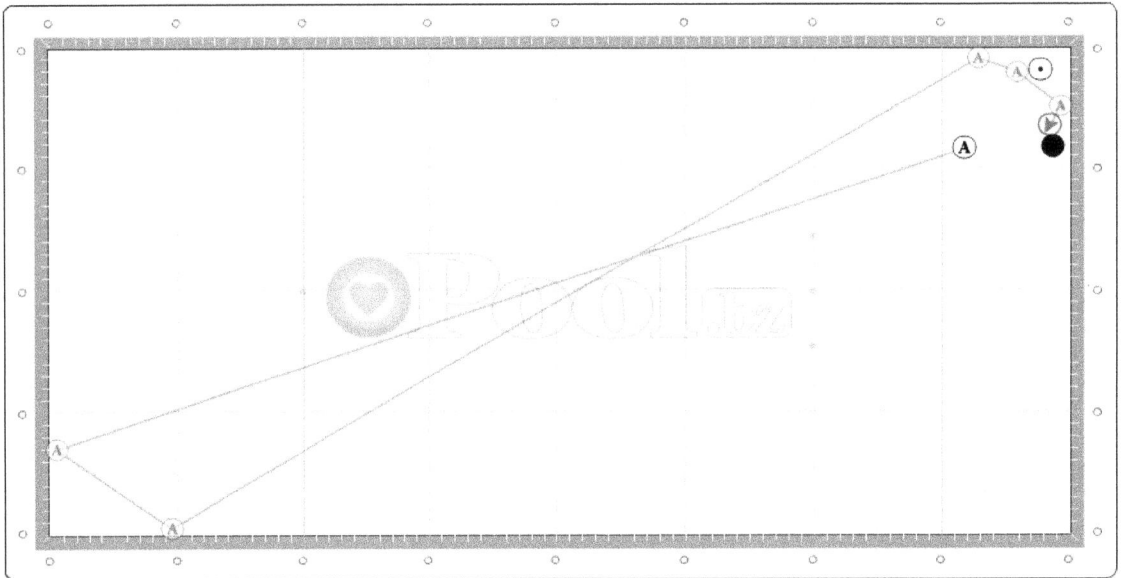

E:6c – Setup

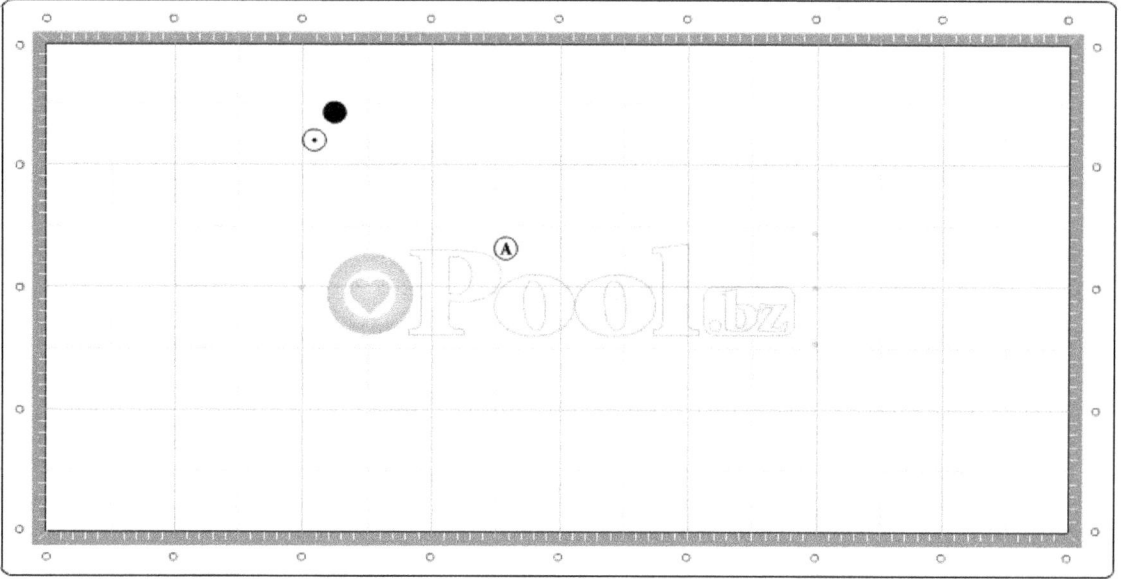

Shot Pattern

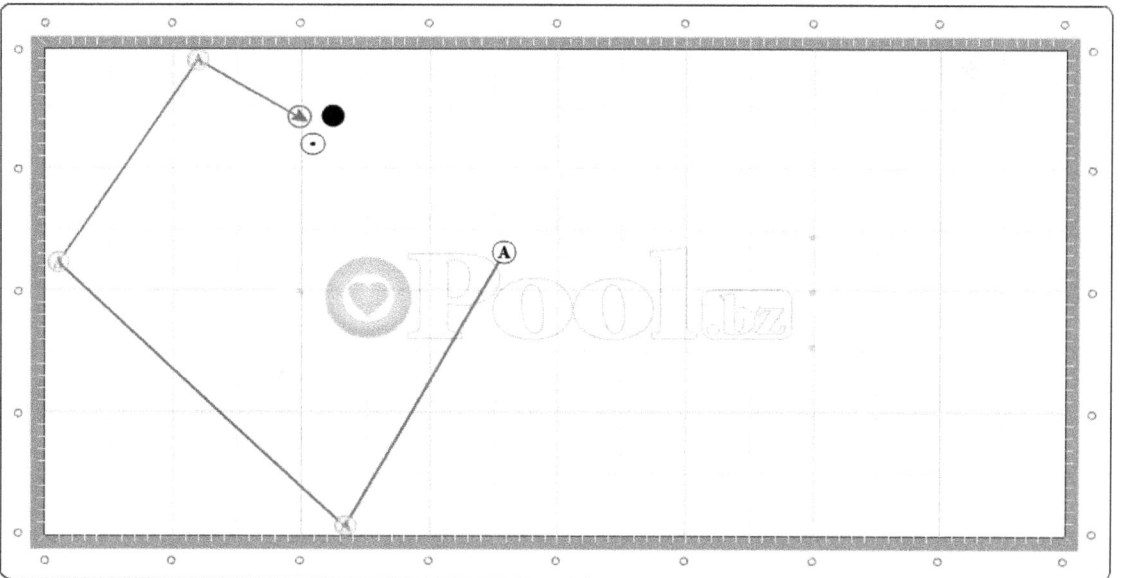

E:6d – Setup

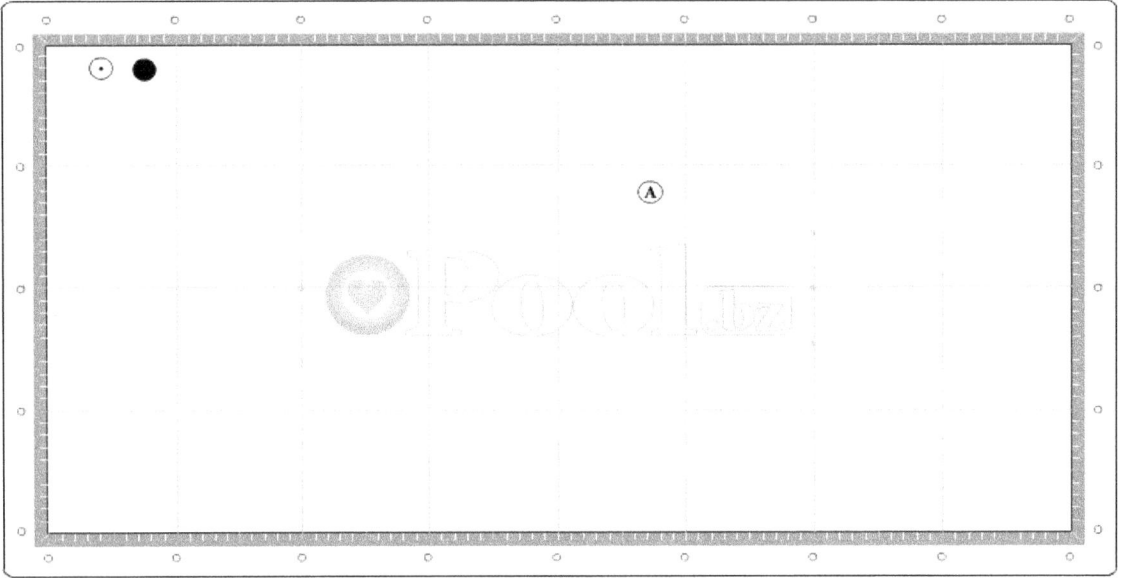

Shot Pattern

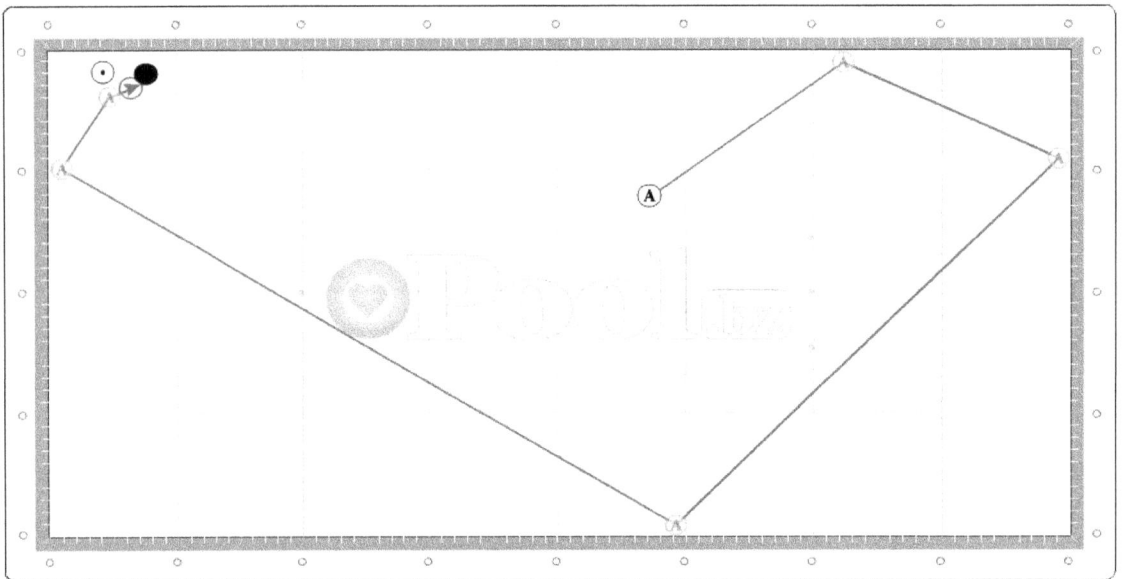

F: 4+ Cushions First

On this set of shots, the player decided to shoot the CB into four (or more) rails before the CB contacts the first OB. For the most part, the fourth rail was more or less accidental, since the OB was close to the cushion. On these shots, the Cue Ball goes four or more rails before it contacts the first Object Ball.

F: Group 1

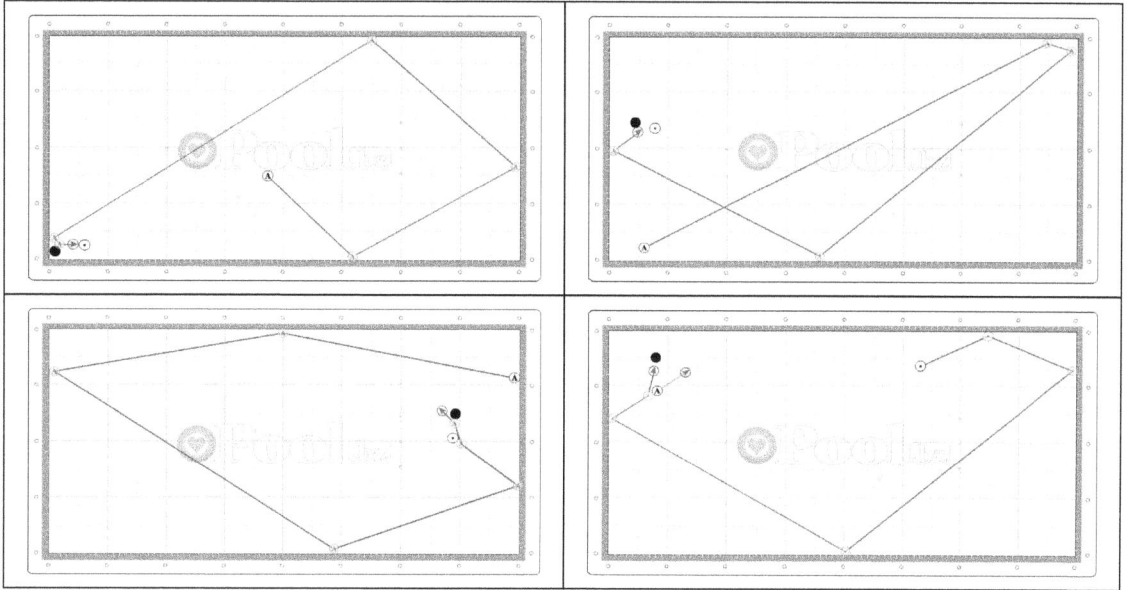

Analysis:

F:1a. _____

F:1b. _____

F:1c. _____

F:1d. _____

F:1a – Setup

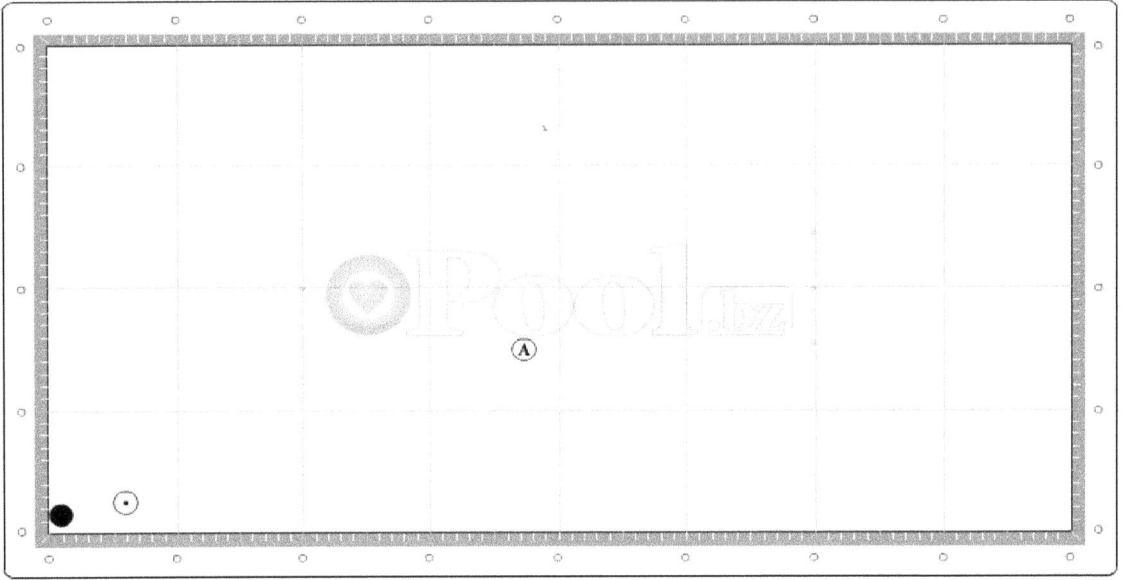

Shot Pattern (4 rails)

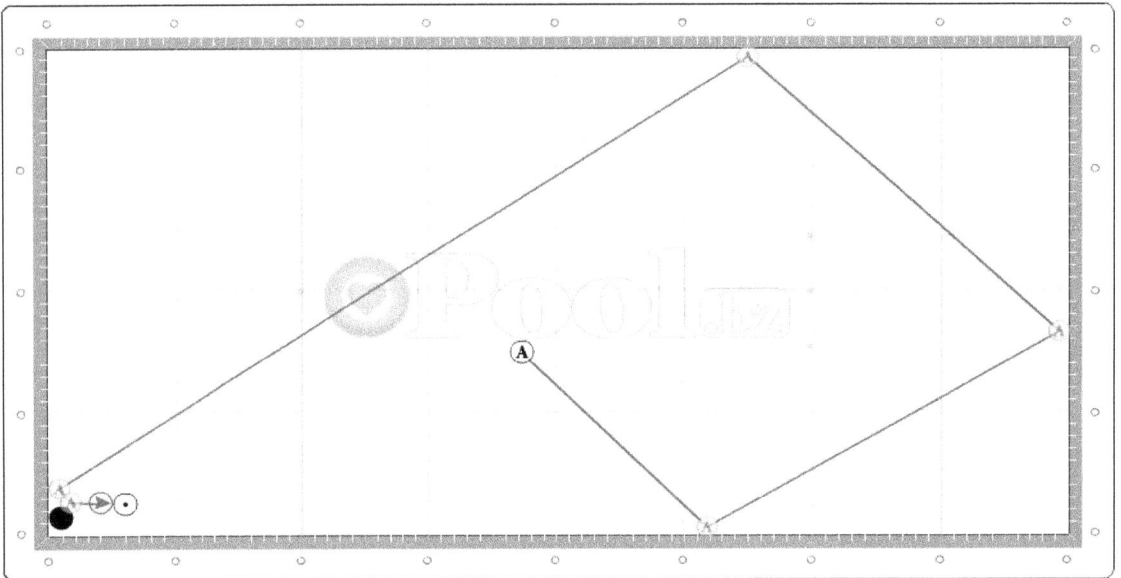

F:1b – Setup

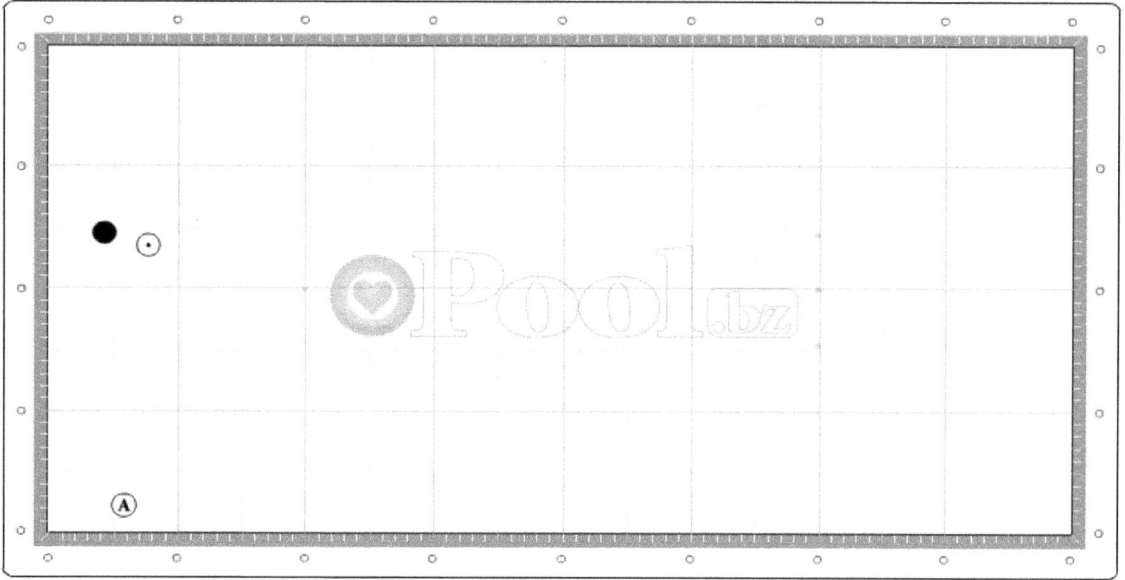

Shot Pattern (4 rails)

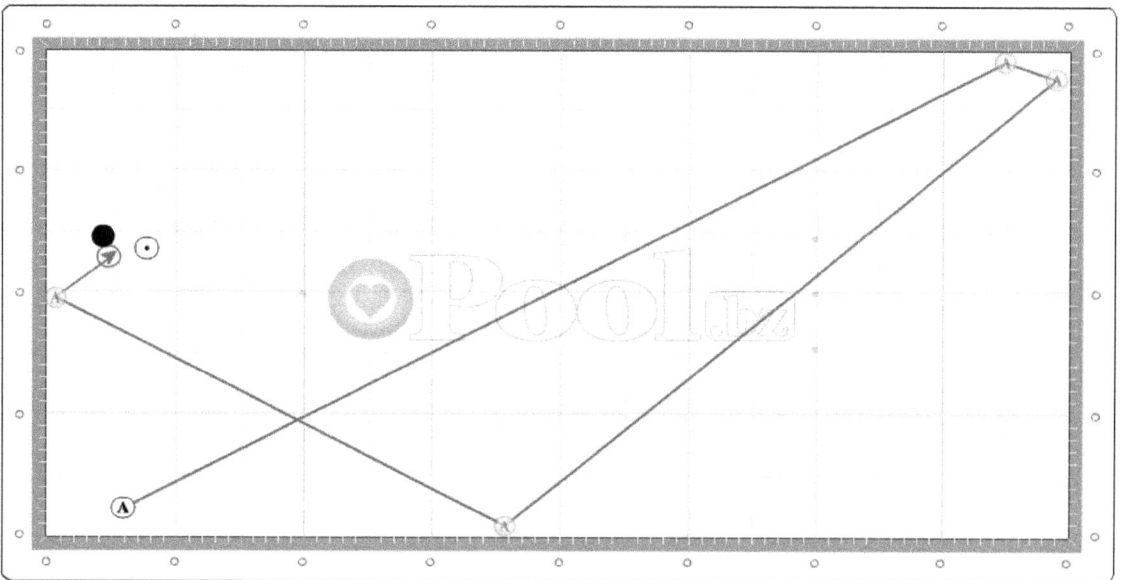

F:1c – Setup

Shot Pattern (4 rails)

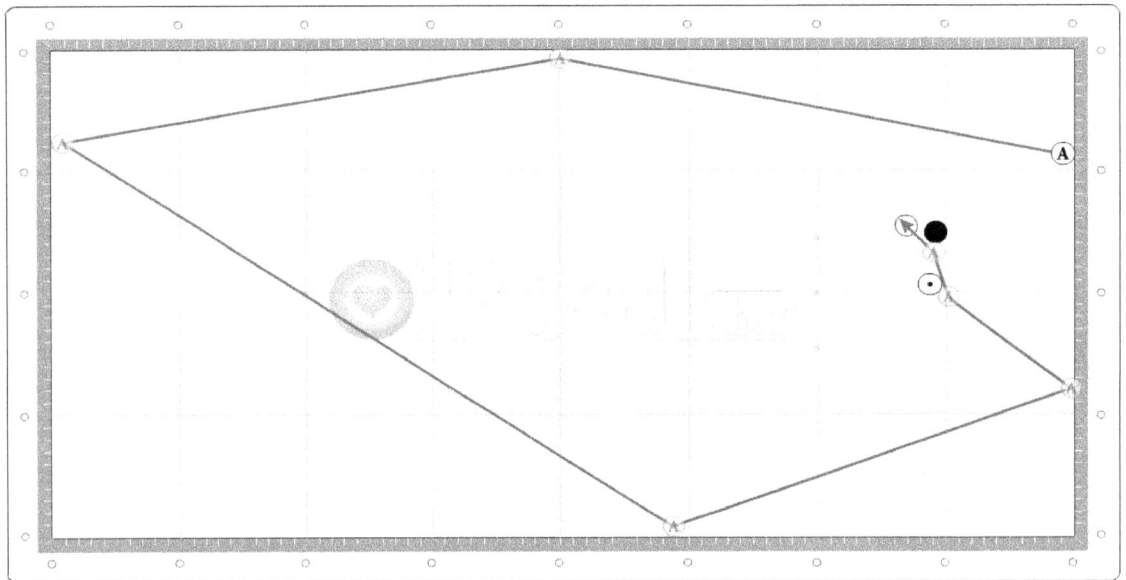

F1d – Setup

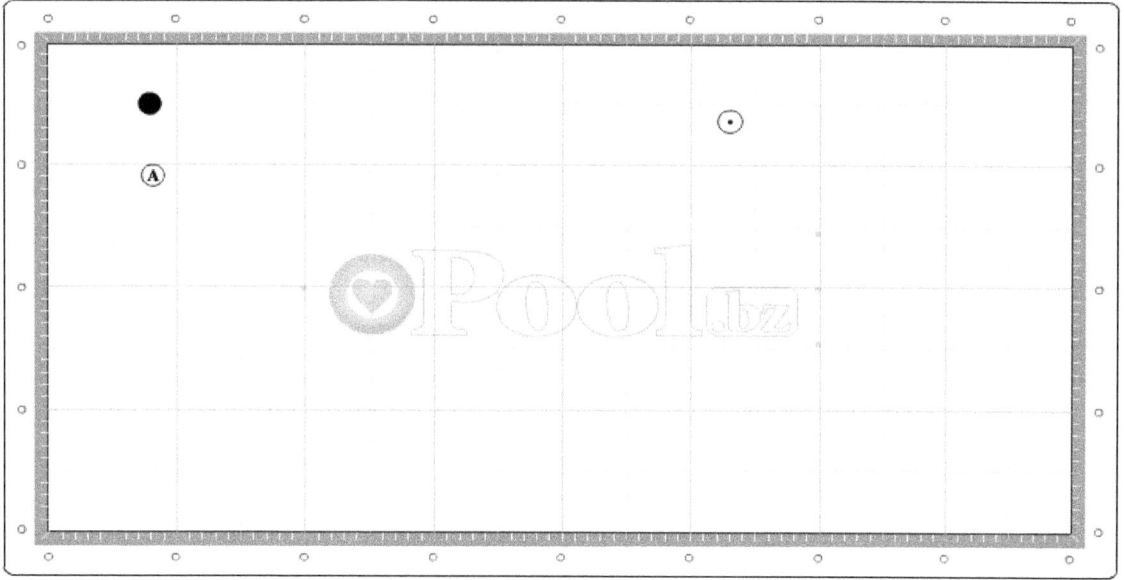

Shot Pattern (4 rails)

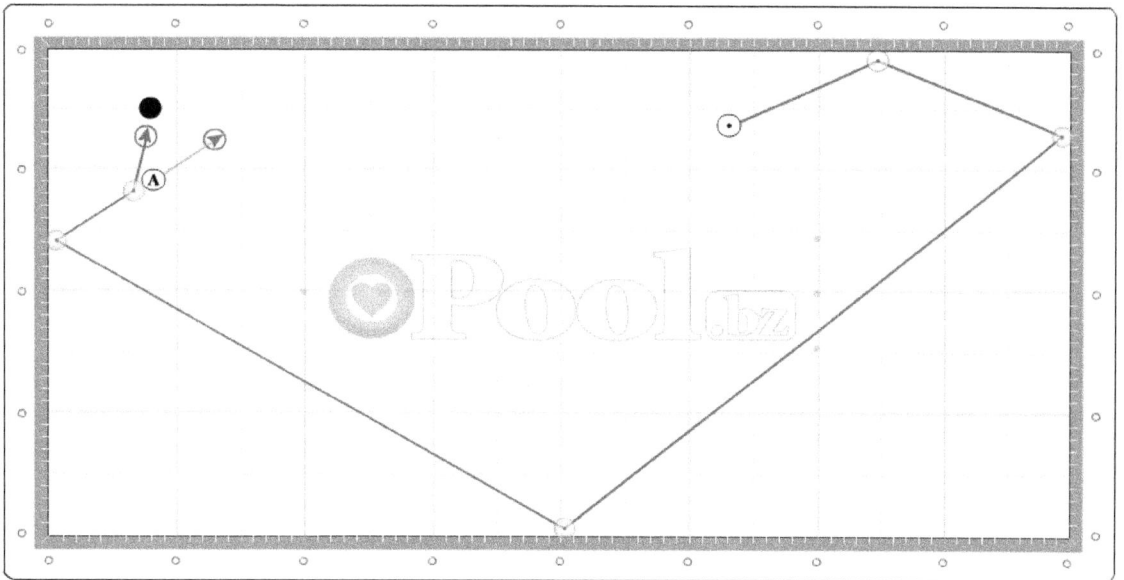

F: Group 2

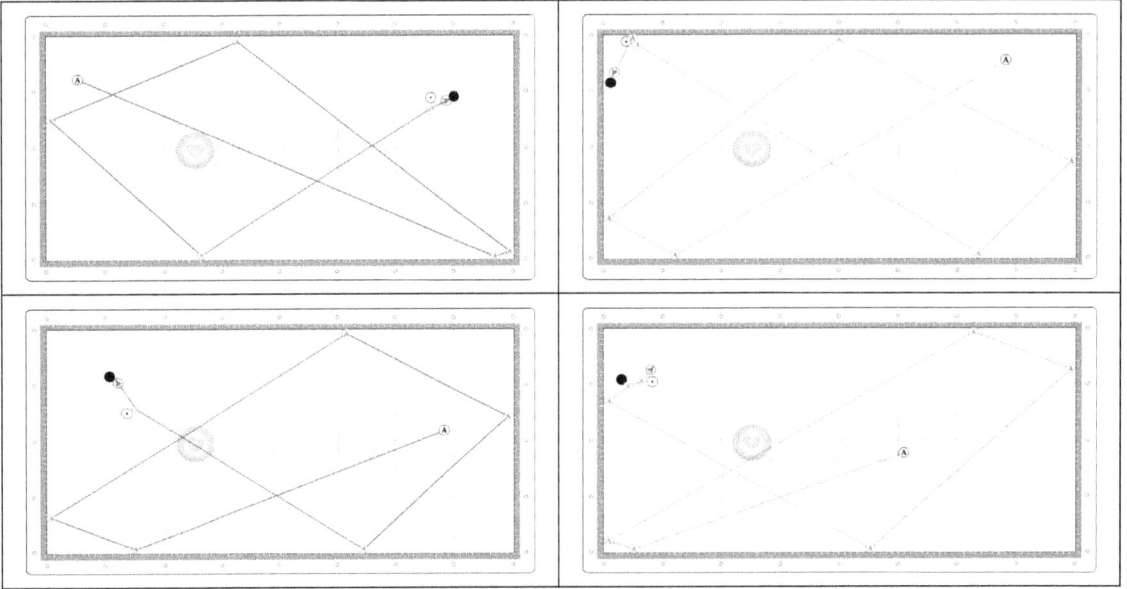

Analysis:

F:2a. _____

F:2b. _____

F:2c. _____

F:2d. _____

F:2a – Setup

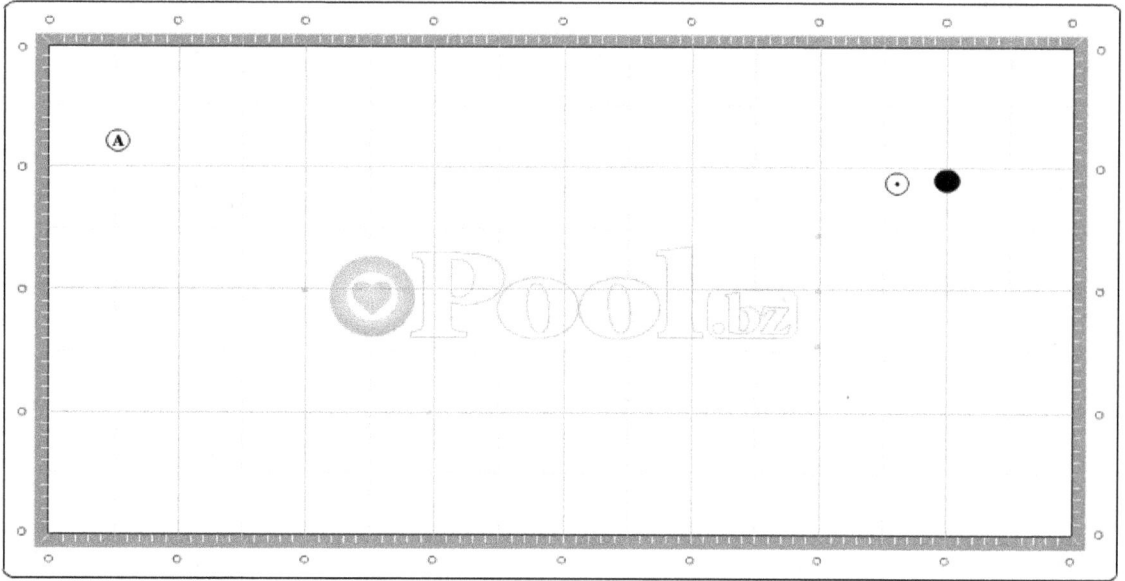

Shot Pattern (5 rails)

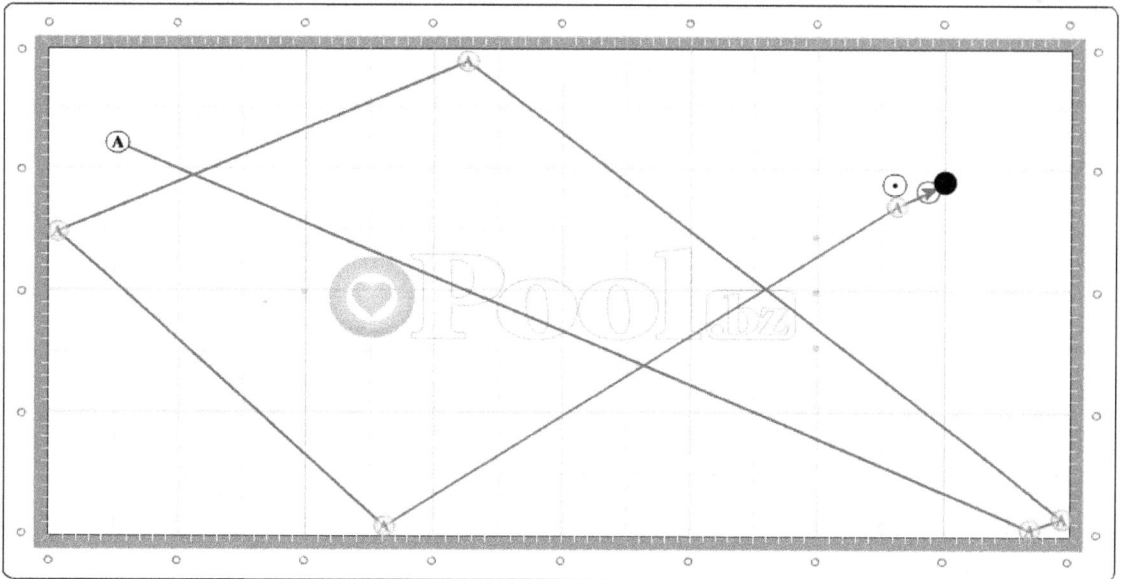

F:2b – Setup

Shot Pattern (5 rails)

F:2c – Setup

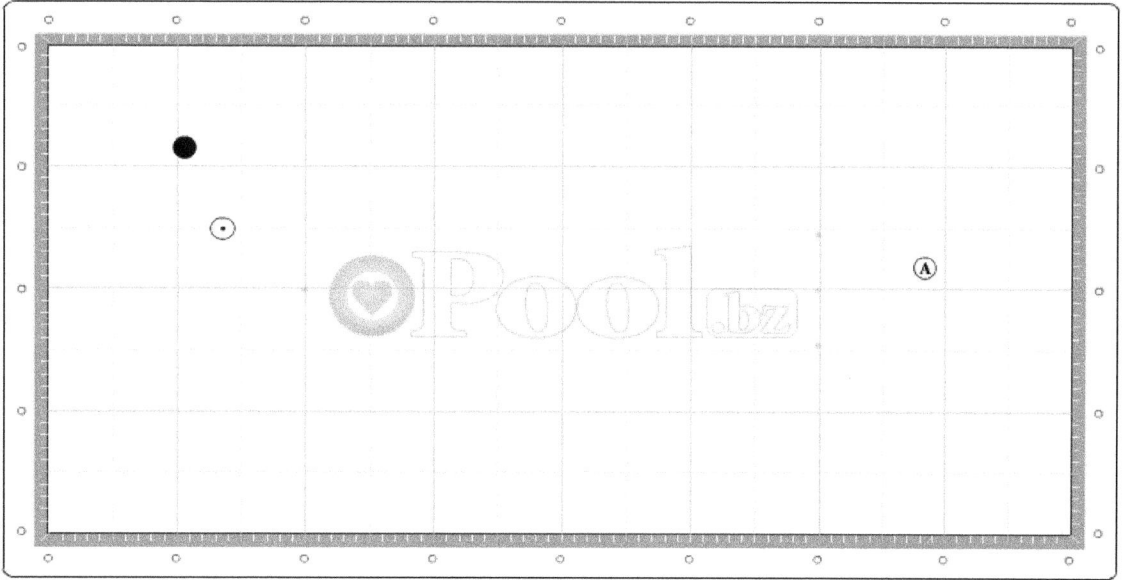

Shot Pattern (5 rails)

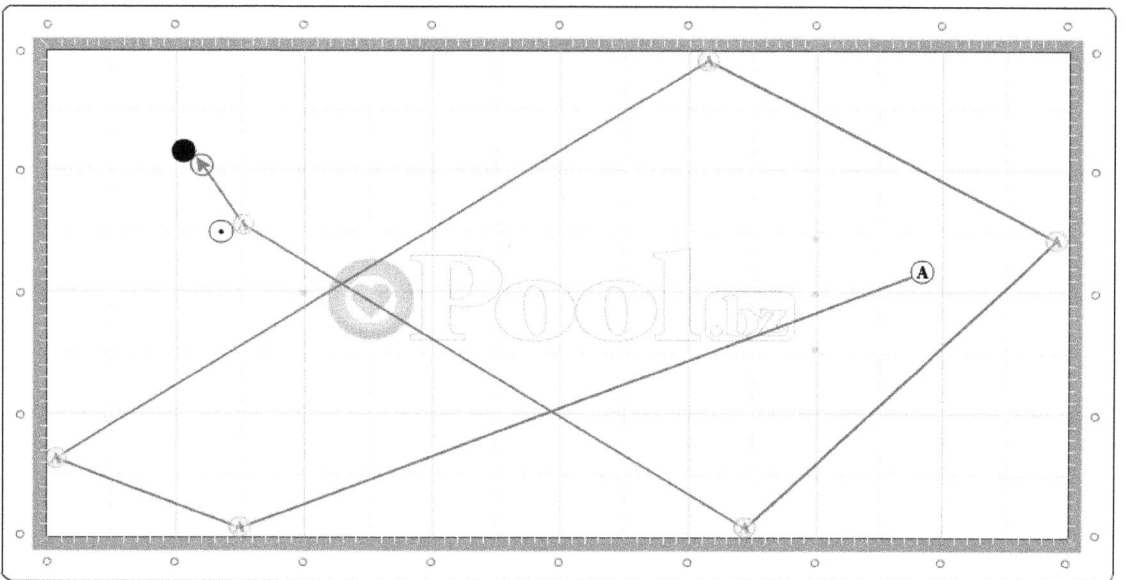

F:2d – Setup

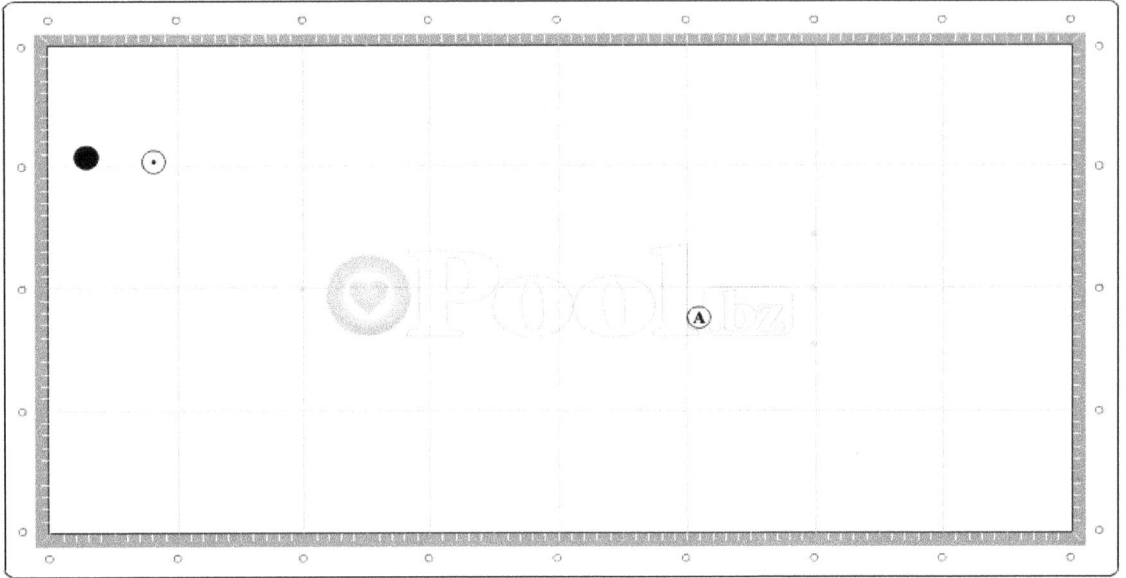

Shot Pattern (6 rails)

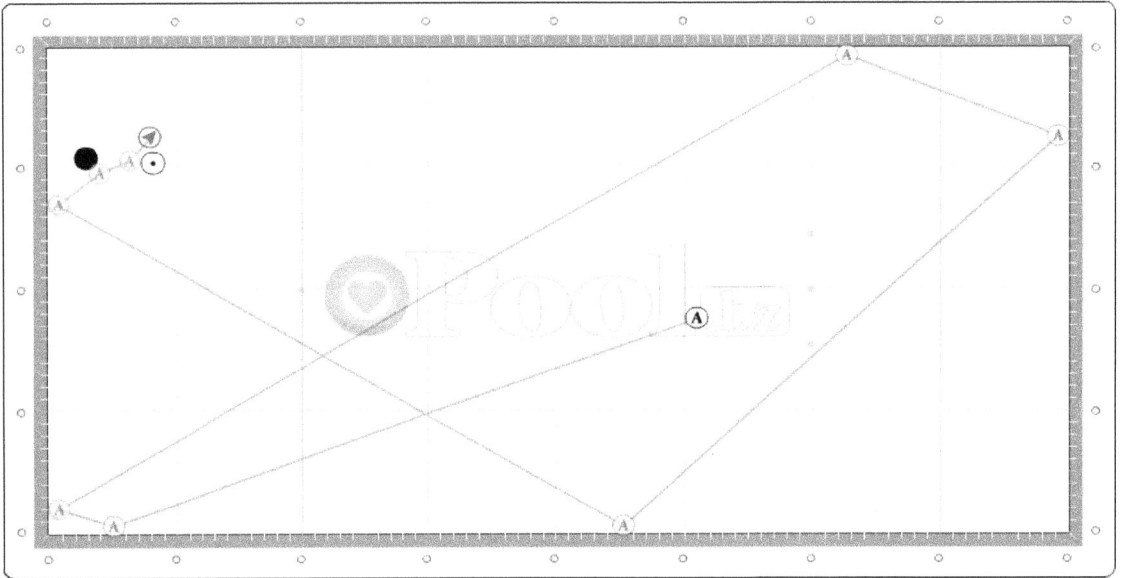